More Miniature Perfume Bottles

Glinda Bowman

77 Lower Valley Road, Atglen, PA 19310

To everyone who is obsessed with miniature perfume bottles.

Copyright © 1996 by Glinda Bowman

Printed in Hong Kong
ISBN: 0-88740-999-7

Back cover author photo: Creative Impression Studio

Library of Congress Cataloging-in-Publication Data

Bowman, Glinda.
  More miniature perfume bottles / Glinda Bowman.
     p.   cm.
  Includes bibliographical references and index.
  ISBN: 0-88740-999-7 (paper)
  1. Miniature perfume bottles--Collectors and collecting--United States--Catalogs. I. Title. II. Title: Miniature perfume bottles
  NK8475.P47B72   1996
  748.8'2'075--dc20   96-20299
                    CIP

Published by Schiffer Publishing Ltd.
77 Lower Valley Road
Atglen, PA 19310
Please write for a free catalog.
This book may be purchased from the publisher.
Please include $2.95 for shipping.
Try your bookstore first.

We are interested in hearing from authors with book ideas on related subjects.

Contents

Acknowledgments

A special "thank you" to everyone who has helped me with this book, including Patricia Bahr, Barbara Bartnicki, Susan Becker, Michele Bowman, Marlene Butts, Linda Collins, Clara Crumbly, Sherry Cvelbar, John & Shelley Davidson, Sung Hye Davidson, Debbie Dearth, Cindy Decker, Lynette Early, Marge Feenerty, Sheri Grove, Mary Ann Hartline, Frances G. Henley, Melissa Jacobs, Jan Lytle, Suzanne Mahley, Mandy Games McDevitt, Betty Sue McNeil, Pam Mueller, Diane Munday, Naomi Palko, Irene Parks, Debbe L, Reames, Nickelyn S. Reames, Nancy Reilly, Susan Sanford, Susan Stubenrod, Barbara Tan, Linda Taylor, Lucille Valentine and Vicki Wright. My husband, John R. Bowman, deserves a grand "thank you" for all the help he gave.

As ever, I am grateful to my publisher Peter Schiffer, my talented editor Leslie J. Bockol, and Doug Congdon-Martin, the professional photographer who continues to take beautiful pictures.

I wish to thank all of the collectors who kindly offered the use of their miniature perfume bottles for my second book. All the offers I had to decline (for now!) were appreciated.

Preface

Hello, my collecting friends! First I want to thank everyone who purchased my previous book, *Miniature Perfume Bottles*. I have been quite pleased to learn that there are many people other than myself who are collecting these beautiful miniature perfume bottles. The trend has finally surfaced, with long-overdue vigor and enthusiasm. The correspondence I have received from you has encouraged me to undertake this second book, which I hope you will enjoy.

In the past, miniature perfume bottles were listed and displayed only alongside larger perfume bottles. Because they compliment perfume bottles of any size so well, they will no doubt continue to be categorized this way. However, miniature perfume bottles are beginning to gain recognition as collectibles in their own right, independent of their larger counterparts. It is exciting to know that *we* are making it happen!

The letters I have received from all of you, my fellow collectors, have been most enjoyable. I apologize for not acknowledging them more quickly, but I did manage to reply to all of them and your patience was appreciated. It has been great hearing from collectors all over the United States.

Quite a few collectors from the United States have traveled to my shop, The Parfum Boutique, to have their books autographed and find new bottles. A truck driver from Illinois stopped while en route to get an autograph for his wife's book. He continues to stop occasionally for new minis for his wife's collection. They both share in the enjoyment of collecting minis, quite a few of which he has found in his travels. Another time, two devoted mini collectors traveled from Virginia to meet me and get their books signed. We talked until midnight, sharing our interest and information on minis. They are as obsessed with collecting minis as I am. Even though they work all week, they get up early on weekends to search local garage sales and flea markets for new minis. They also plan short trips to outlying areas to find even more. It was a pleasure talking to them since we had much to share on the subject.

I have also heard from miniature perfume bottle collectors around the world, and have found that collectors in Europe and elsewhere in the world are just as devoted as are collectors in the United States. There seems to be a larger selection of miniatures available in Europe, probably since many parfumeries are located there. Europe's perfume bottle flea markets would make any collector eager to explore. The prices are higher in Europe for miniature perfume bottles due to the strong interest in collecting. It is fun being a part of such a devoted group of collectors!

I suggest that you build yourself a library of information on miniatures, including my book *Miniature Perfume Bottles*. The information and pictures will be convenient for quick reference when on mini searches. These books lists many old and beautiful minis which are still available on the collectors' market. Remember, if I can find them, so can you! I am sure that there are many beautiful minis still waiting to be found.

I would enjoy hearing from you, my fellow collectors. Please direct all correspondence to me, Glinda Bowman, 515 Fairmont Avenue, Wheeling, West Virginia, 26003. Let's keep the miniature perfume bottle collecting trend on top...after all, we've come a long way, MINI!

What is a Miniature Perfume Bottle?

Miniatures are smaller versions of larger fragrance bottles. They range from 1.87ml (1/16oz.) to 7.5ml (1/4oz.), with slight variations. I have provided both measurements for each bottle wherever possible, but you may find this table of conversions useful nonetheless:

NOTE: Sometimes the bottle-size conversions in captions will be inconsistent. This is because they were taken directly from the box, and manufacturers sometimes used approximations. For example, one manufacturer may have considered 2ml equal to 1/16 oz., while another used the more accurate 1.87ml measurement.

METRIC CONVERSION TABLE EQUIVALENTS OF COMMON PERFUME BOTTLES

(ml = millilitre; oz. = ounce)

1.87ml	.0625oz.	1/16oz.	1/2dram
3ml	.10oz.		
3.75ml	.125oz.	1/8oz.	1 dram
4ml	.13oz.		
5ml	.16oz.	1/6oz.	
6ml	.20oz.		
7.5ml	.25oz.	1/4oz.	2 drams
10ml	.333oz.	1/3oz.	
15ml	.5oz.	1/2oz.	
22.5ml	.75oz.	3/4oz.	6 drams
30ml	1oz.		
40ml	1.33oz.		
50ml	1.7oz.		8 drams
60ml	2oz.	1/16 litre	

Miniature Bottles From Decades Past

In addition to showing bottles from recent years, I decided to list a wide variety of older minis since many collectors expressed an interest in them. I sought out and found many old and unique minis from the 1920s, '30s and '40s that bear witness to the trendy bottle designs by perfume companies in years past.

Many times, older minis are found to be in a condition that is unattractive due to age and treatment. These beautiful old minis are quite interesting and may require some "tender loving care" in order to shine again, but they are well worth the work. Don't hesitate in adding them to your collection! It's a challenge to take an old mini that has seen better days and bring back some of its lost beauty. Collecting old minis saves them from being tossed on the junk pile, preserving them for future reference so others can enjoy them. Do a good deed: save a mini in need!

Some of the older minis that I found were in excellent condition, with unbroken seals — but a considerable amount of the fragrance had nonetheless evaporated. This does not seem possible if the bottle has never been opened, but it is. In time, the alcohol does evaporate, leaving a concentrated oil base that eventually dries up. After a period of time, any fragrance will become discolored and evaporate, but the bottle remains the collectible, whether full or empty. Therefore, it is best to use a new fragrance and collect the pretty bottle. Expect to pay full market value for new minis that are filled with a fresh fragrance.

If you are fortunate enough to find a mini with the original box, by all means keep the box! It *does* increase the value, and you can expect to pay more for it. On the other hand, many older minis may not come with a box, but that doesn't mean you should pass them up. After all, the bottle can stand alone as a collectible, whereas the box cannot.

I have acquired an interest in old minis and hope other collectors enjoy seeing many of the styles and designs that were popular in the past. Older bottle designs have wondeful details, individual trademarks of beauty that can be attributed to the skilled artisans that created them. Many of these bottle designers never received the recognition they deserve for their creations, especially if the fragrance did not become popular. To make up for it, let's offer a grand salute to all the artisans of the past who created beautiful perfume bottles for us to enjoy today!

In Quest of Minis

The best part of any mini search is finding a new addition, but sometimes the search itself can be just as much fun. I have had some unforgetable encounters, both humorous and serious, some of which I will share with you . I hope everyone can relate to some of these occasions and find some amusement in them. Surely, I'm not the only collector who has memorable mini searches!

It has proven to be worthwhile for me to travel within a 200 to 300 mile radius (300 to 500 kilometers) from my home in order to search for minis. It surely suggests "mini mania" when I leave early on Sunday mornings, drive for two to three hours to flea markets and antique shops, then walk four to five hours searching, perhaps in the hot sun, rain or cold, to find new minis — but finding one more unique example makes it worth all the effort. By chance, I have been very fortunate in acquiring a sizeable amount of old minis from private individuals. The following mini search has proven to be my most productive (and favorite) trip thus far.

One particular Sunday, my husband and I decided to spend the day searching for minis in antique shops in the Uniontown, Pennsylvania, area on Route 40, known as "Old National Road." In the 1950s, this antique shop route attracted collectors and tourists; despite new interstate highways, many of the antique shops remain in business today.

We stopped at many shops with no luck — one dealer had never heard of minis, let alone ever seen one! When antique dealers have no minis, I always ask if they know anyone else who may have some for sale. In the very last antique shop, the dealer referred me to a lady in the area who had collected mini perfume bottles for years, though he didn't know if she wanted to sell them. We felt that it was worth a drive to her home.

After explaining to the lady's husband why we were there, he told us that she had not been feeling well for several days, but he would ask if she felt well enough to talk to us. She kindly agreed and invited us into their home — what a great lady! I told her about my first book and explained that I needed minis for a second one. This lady had collected regular-size perfume bottles as well as miniatures, putting the minis away in boxes except for the few favorites she wanted to display. She agreed to let me purchase some of her minis if I would give her a week or more to get them together. Needless to say, I was extremely happy on the ride home, and waited anxiously for the return visit. Thanks to her, I purchased over seventy-five old and unique minis from the 1920s, '30s, and '40s. I have returned to her home several more times and acquired an impressive amount of unusual minis from her. These miniature perfume bottles are among my most treasured, and some are pictured in this book for you to enjoy. This wonderful friend continues to search for miniature perfume bottles for my collection, and I anxiously await another visit. You can see why this is my favorite mini search!

On another occasion, a lady approached me at a book signing at a local mall bookstore. She wanted to know if I would be interested in some old minis that had recently been left to her by a family friend. Although she had admired them as a young girl, she did not wish to collect them — but I could hardly wait to see them. Three weeks later I purchased about thirty-five unusual minis from her. Months later, I visited her home and purchased three boxes of a variety of minis and regular sized perfumes. Thanks to her, I can share these old and unique minis with everyone. These rare occasions make up for all the searches that took hours of walking in order to produce a single mini. As you know, large quanities are not always this easy to find; they are a collector's dream come true. I appreciate her generosity.

Have you ever found a mini that you had been intensely searching for, only to discover that you didn't have enough cash with you to purchase it? What a terrible feeling! My husband, a salesman who travels a 200 mile (350 km) radius from our home, had that happen to him. One Friday, he had some free time to stop at a flea market and search for minis. He did not have a large sum of money with him that day, but wanted to suprise me with a few new minis, if possible. Lo and behold, a lady had a mini that I had wanted for a long time; he knew he couldn't go home without it. The price was right, just twenty-five dollars, but he had only eighteen dollars cash with him. How do you buy something you desperately want when you don't have enough money? You think fast for a possible solution. My husband decided to humble himself and explain to the lady that he wanted that mini desperately. He told her that her price was right, but he only had eighteen dollars with him. Would she please accept that amount for the mini?

After a tense moment of waiting, she agreed. Was it the desperate look on his face or the pleading look in his eyes? We will never know. Whatever the reason, I'm sure she doesn't get that type of buying approach very often. My husband was elated with his little treasure and it was a super suprise for me. He deserves a star for saving the day — oops, I mean for saving the *mini!*

Have you ever watched a beautiful mini slip through your hands — or the hands of the seller — before you could purchase it? It happened to me at a flea market one Sunday. Mini bottles were somewhat scarce that hot July day; though we had walked for hours, covering over half of the market area, we had only found a few minis. Finally I spotted a box full of them, and rushed over with a great feeling of relief. I rummaged through the box and found a few nice ones, including one delicate old bottle in great condition with the label intact. With this find, I thought to

myself, "This was a productive day after all." I handed the bottles to the seller to wrap while I got the money to pay him.

Suddenly, there was a crash. I heard glass breaking on the pavement. My heart fell to my feet as I looked up to see that he had dropped one mini bottle. As you can guess, he had dropped the unique mini I had wanted most. Needless to say, I was quite disappointed, but tried to accept his apology with dignity. What a tragedy to witness. What was once a unique find was swept up and thrown away, its beauty never again to be enjoyed. Now, when handing a mini to the seller, I hold the bottle tightly until it is properly taken from my hand, and I remind them to be careful with it. Indeed, I have learned from that experience.

Sometimes, I have found, it is worth looking beyond the regular display tables! At a local antique market on a rainy Sunday morning, I spotted a large box full of minis stacked on top of other boxes in the back seat of a station wagon. The lady was not unloading the boxes because of the pouring rain. With my mouth watering in anticipation, I felt like a child looking into a display case full of candy. But it looked as though she might be leaving! I wanted to see those minis if at all possible, so I asked her. She agreed. I stood awkwardly searching the box in the car, while my husband tried to hold an umbrella with one hand and minis in the other. I definitely did not want to overlook a new mini for my collection! It took a while to search the box, but I found fifteen new minis, so it was all worth a little rain.

Whether there is sun, heat, rain, wind, cold, or snow, when it comes to finding a new mini, nothing humanly bearable stops my search. Let me find one precious new mini for my collection and I consider it all worthwhile. These mini searches have been fun, and I have learned many things from them. If you have any episodes to share, please write — I would enjoy hearing about *your* experiences.

Bottle Designers & Manufacturers

As you collect the miniature fragrances, you will notice that most of the bottles produced are European, just as most of the fragrance trade is European. Some of the small bottles are produced by glass works that have survived for centuries. Many of the bottles were designed by outside artists, while some bottle glassworks furnished their own designs. The first bottle factory in France was established in 1290. Not surprisingly, many of the bottles you find will have the trademarks (usually on the bottom) of French companies.

The Pochet et du Courval Glass Company in France dates back to the 1600s, and probably makes most of the mimiature perfume bottles that are on the market today. The company makes bottles for Balmain, Dior, Patou, and Cartier, to name a few. Its trademark is "HP."

Saint Govain Desjonqueres, also dating from the 1600s, is another large producer of modern perfume bottles. Today, it makes bottles for Balmain, Lancome, Roger and Gallet, and Gucci, among others. Its trademark is "SGD" OR "S."

The Verreries Brosse Glass Firm, owned by E. Barre, has designed and manufactured many scent bottles. Two popular examples are APRIL SHOWERS by Cheramy and Coco Chanel's CHANEL NO 5. Verreries Brosse's trademard is "VB/BR."

The Dinand workshop is a leading bottle maker today. Pierre Dinand has designed bottles for Krizia and Givenchy.

The Wheaton Glass Company is a popular American glass factory that has manufactured perfume bottles for American and European perfumers. It has also made bottles for Avon. EVENING IN PARIS, by Bourjois, is a popular bottle you can find today with the Wheaton Glass Company trademark, a "W" in a circle.

In the early 1900s, Francis Coty secured the talents of René Lalique to design commercial bottles for his scents, thereby revolutionizing the scent trade. René Lalique also manufactured bottles with semi-automation, making them more affordable. He continued in the glass business with much success, designing and manufacturing bottles for Coty, Guerlain, and Molinard, among others. René Lalique's trademark is "RL" or "Lalique."

To this day, the firm is controlled by the Lalique family. René's son Marc Lalique has designed bottles for Jeanne Lancome, Raphael, Nina Ricci, Rochas, and many others. The fragrance LALIQUE, introduced in 1992 by Marie-Claude Lalique of Lalique Parfums, comes in a Lalique-designed bottle.

KANTARA eau de toilette by Albin du Roy. Paris, France. The twisted bottle is a replica of the larger original. 4ml (.14oz.).

CASAQUE parfum by the firm of Jean D'Albret, established in 1946 in Paris, France. The fragrance was introduced in 1957. 1.87ml (1/16oz.).

LOVE parfum by A H R C. Brookville, U.S.A. The 15ml (1/2oz.) clear glass bottle has the "HP" Pochet et du Courval trademark.

GOLD SATIN perfume by Angelique. Wilton, CT. Distributed from NY, NY. The 3.75ml (1/8oz.) gold-capped bottle sits in a gold metal base. The bottle is carried in a gold metal case. The bottle dates from the 1950s.

WHITE SATIN perfume by Angelique. Wilton, CT. The 3.75ml (1/8oz.) bottle dates from 1949.

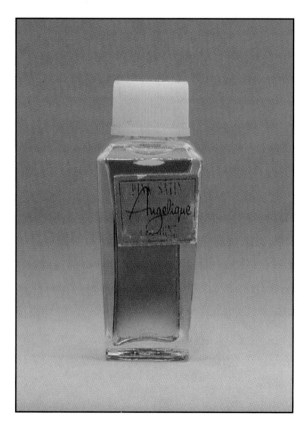

DALINI eau de parfum by Anucci. The 7.5ml (1/4oz.) frosted glass bottle is marked "DALINI" in gold letters.

PINK SATIN cologne by Angelique, established in 1946 in Wilton, CT. The 3.75ml (1/8oz.) bottle dates from the 1950s.

ORANGE BLOSSOMS perfume by Annette. Paris, France. NY, NY. The bottle has a cork stopper and a brass cap. 15ml (1/2oz.).

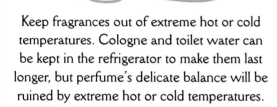

Keep fragrances out of extreme hot or cold temperatures. Cologne and toilet water can be kept in the refrigerator to make them last longer, but perfume's delicate balance will be ruined by extreme hot or cold temperatures.

BLUE GRASS parfum by Elizabeth Arden Co., established in 1915. NY, NY. The floral-ambery fragrance created in 1934 is contained in a 6ml (.2oz.) bottle and was her best selling perfume.

TUSCANY PER DONNA parfum by Aramis Inc. NY, NY. Distributed by Estee Lauder. The floral-oriental fragrance created by Aramis in 1993 is contained in a 3.5ml (.12oz.) bottle.

BLUE GRASS perfume essence by Elizabeth Arden Co. NY, NY. The 7.5ml (1/4oz.) bottle was made in Italy.

OPERA 450 flower mist by Elizabeth Arden Co. NY, NY. "ARDEN" is molded into the bottom of the 15ml (1/2oz.) bottle. 450 was the number of Elizabeth Arden's opera box in the 1940s, the decade from which this bottle originates.

CABRIOLE — more than a cologne — by Elizabeth Arden Co. NY, NY. 3.75ml (1/8oz.).

RED DOOR parfum by Elizabeth Arden Co. NY, NY. The floral-ambery fragrance was created in 1989 and is contained in a 5ml (.17oz.) bottle.

SUNFLOWERS eau de toilette by Elizabeth Arden Co. NY, NY. The floral-fruity fragrance introduced in 1993 is contained in a 7.5ml (1/4oz.) bottle.

TRUE LOVE parfum by Elizabeth Arden Co. NY, NY. The stopper of the 3.7ml (.12oz.) bottle has two entwined rings in gold.

GIO de Giorgio Armani eau de parfum. Distributed by Giorgio Armani Parfums. Division of Cosmair Inc. NY, NY. The 1993 floral-fruity fragrance is contained in a 5ml (.17oz.) bottle.

GARDENIA perfume by Ashley. NY, NY. 7.5ml (1/4oz.)

SHEE-GWEE perfume by Melina. Created and manfactured by M. Atkins Ltd. Republic of Ireland. 7.5ml (1/4oz.) "Shee-Gwee" is the Gaelic word meaning 'The Enchanted Breeze' The Shee were the little people of Irish folklore. The fragrance is tinted green.

JODELLE perfume by Associated Merchandising Corp. in 1927. NY, NY. The 3.75ml (1/8oz.) bottle is from the 1930s.

Left: CHEN YU-FLOWERING ALMOND perfume by Associated Distributor Inc. in 1938. Chicago, IL. 7.5ml (1/4oz.)

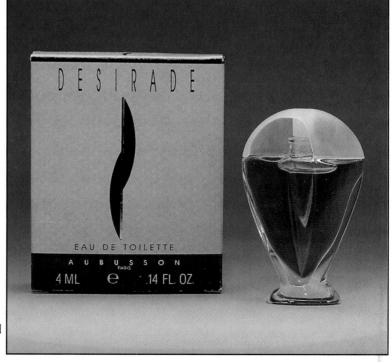

Right:DESIRADE eau de toilette by Parfums Aubusson. Paris, France. "DESIRADE," the essence of desire, is a floral semi-oriental fragrance introduced in 1990 and contained in a 4ml (.14oz.) bottle.

LORE perfume by Babcock. NY, NY. The firm of A.P. Babcock dates back to the late 1800s. The 3.75ml (1/8oz.) blue-capped bottle dates from the 1930s.

LE DIX parfum by Cristobal Balenciaga. The couture house was established in Paris, France in 1937. The floral-aldehyde fragrance was introduced in 1947. The Pochet et du Courval bottle is 1.87ml (1/16oz.)

Below: SONATA parfum by J.S. Bach. Italy. 7.5ml (1/4oz.)

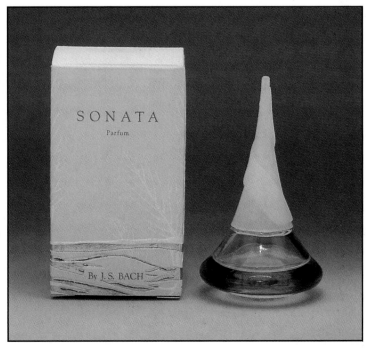

OH LA LA eau de parfum by Loris Azzaro. Paris, France. 3ml (.1oz.) "Delicious, lively, oriental. That's my dream perfume for you," proclaimed Loris Azzaro in 1993. The bottle sits upside-down in a lovely plastic display. "A" is on the gold cap. The bottle is designed like a Venetian wine glass. A Serge Mansau design.

JOLIE MADAME parfum by Parfums Balmain. Pierre Balmain established his couture house in 1945 in Paris, France. The chypre-floral animalic fragrance was introduced in 1953. "FRANCE" is molded into the bottom of the 1.87ml (1/16oz.) bottle.

QUADRILLE parfum by Cristobal Balenciaga. Paris, France. The floral fragrance was introduced in 1955 and is contained in a "HP" fluted glass bottle. A double "B" is on the cap. 3.75ml (1/8oz.).

MISHA parfum by Parfums Mikhail Baryshinikov. NY, NY. Richard Barrie Fragrances, Inc. Distributed from East Hampton, NY. 5ml (.16oz.). The fragrance is a chypre-floral animalic.

BIBI eau de toilette de Jean Barthet. Parfums Jean Barthet. Paris, France. The 7ml (.24oz.) bottle has "HP MADE IN FRANCE" molded into the bottom and "BIBI" with stylized initials in raised letters on the front. A chypre-floral fragrance

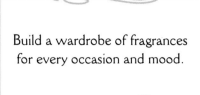

Build a wardrobe of fragrances for every occasion and mood.

Above: HENRI BENDEL parfum by Henri Bendel. Distributed in the U.S.A. by Gryphon Dev. NY, NY. 4ml (.13oz.)

Above: VISION NOIR eau de parfum de Robert Beaulieu Parfums. Paris, France. The black 7.5ml (1/4oz.) bottle has a fur-covered cap and the initials "RB" on it.

Right: BENDELILAS perfume. Made exclusively for Henri Bendel. Henry Bendel opened a fine store on West 57th Street in New York City in 1912, and introduced perfumes in 1915. The squared glass bottle has a purple ribbon tied to its neck. Marked 4 drams. 15ml (1/2oz.)

MEMORIES perfume by Bernard Perfumer. St. Louis, MO. 1.87ml (1/16oz.).

SUEDE perfume by Henri Bendel, introduced in 1938. NY, NY and Paris, France. The gold-cased glass bottle, imported from France in the 1960s, holds 1 dram (3.75ml, or 1/8oz.)

COEUR DE CANANGA ("the heart of Canaga") super concentrate parfum by Franka M. Berger. France. According to the box, it is "from the heart of the flower," by Franka M. Berger. 2ml (1/15oz.)

TORTUE parfum by Poly Bergen Cosmetics. Toronto, Ontario. This fragrance was introduced in 1969. 7ml (1/4oz.).

BAVARDAGE parfum by A. Blanc.
Paris, France. The 1.87ml (1/16oz.)
bottle has "FRANCE" on the
bottom.

VENEZIA eau de toilette by fashion designer Laura Biagiotti.
Milan, Italy. Distributed by Eurocos. Hunt Valley, MD. The
floral-oriental fragrance, introduced in 1992, is contained in a
5ml (.17oz.) bottle.

LA DEB perfume by Blair. Lynchburg, VA. 7.5ml
(1/4oz.). A circled "S" is molded into the bottom of
the bottle.

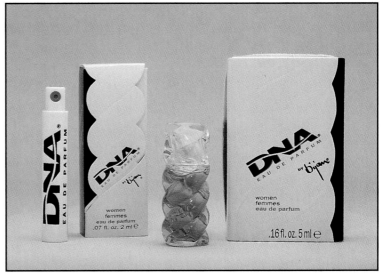

DNA eau de parfum by Bijan. Distributed by Bijan Fragrances.
Beverly Hills, CA. The spiraled bottle contains a floral-ambery
fragrance introduced in 1993. The 5ml (.16oz.) bottle comes
in a unique Bijan box, which reads: "A flamboyant naturelle";
"Open the box and see"; "Love, love more, laugh, cry, dare,
feel everything." Shown with the 2ml (.07oz.) spray vial.
D.N.A. are the initials of Bijan's children, Daniela, Nicolas, and
Alexandra.

ORANGE BLOSSOM perfume by Bo-Kay Perfumer. Jacksonville, FL. The fragrance contained in a 3.75ml (1/8oz.) bottle was introduced in 1924.

BONJOUR eau de parfum by Bonjour Parfums, Inc. Distributed from NY, NY. A plain frosted bottle with a black cap. 7ml (1/4oz.)

MY DESIRE perfume by Bo-Kay Perfumer. Jacksonville, FL. 3.75ml (1/8oz.)

CITANA parfum by A. Blanc. Paris, France. The 2.4ml (.08oz.) bottle is a sunburst design.

EVENING IN PARIS perfume by Bourjois. NY, NY. 5ml (.15oz.) A gold label and a gold cap. "BOURJOIS" appears on the bottom of the bottle.

EVENING IN PARIS perfume by Bourjois, which was founded in Paris in 1860. The cobalt blue bottle holds 3.75ml (1 dram, or 1/8oz.). EVENING IN PARIS, introduced in 1928, is probably the best selling fragrance ever. A circled "W" is on the bottom of the bottle.

EVENING IN PARIS perfume by Bourjois. NY, NY. A 7.5ml (1/4oz.) bottle with a white Bakelite cap.

THEOSIRIS parfum by Guy Bouchara. Paris, France. The 5ml (.16oz.) bottle is gold-painted with a black stopper.

EVENING IN PARIS perfume by Bourjois. NY, NY. A clear bottle with a gold cap and black painted lettering. 7.5ml (1/4oz.).

Above: EVENING IN PARIS perfume by Bourjois. NY, NY. Two bottles, each holding 3.75ml (1/8oz.), one with a gold cap and one with a silver cap.

Left: EVENING IN PARIS perfume by Bourjois. NY, NY. Two cobalt blue bottles with black tasseled caps. 7.5ml (1/4oz.).

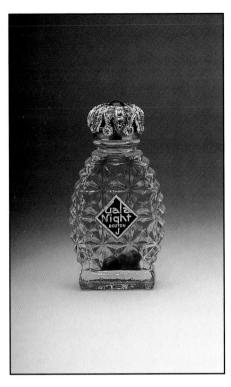

GALA NIGHT
perfume, by Bouton
or the George W.
Button Co. NY, NY.
The fragrance was
introduced in 1928.
The cap has a pink
jewel in the center.
5ml (1/6oz.).

ON THE WIND
cologne parfumee
by Bourjois. NY,
NY. 15ml (1/2oz.).

Left: LILY perfume by Bouton. NY, NY. The label states that
one drop lasts 3 days. The 1.87ml (1/16oz.) bottle is from the
1930s.

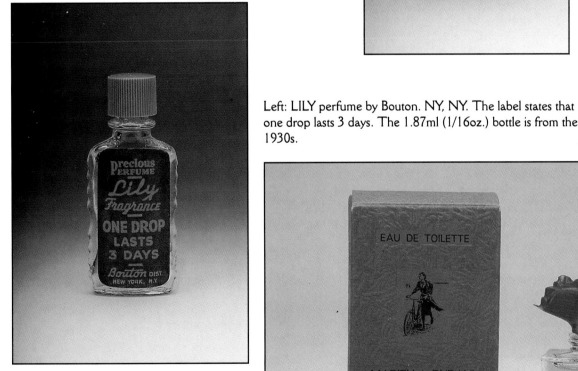

Right: MARIELLA BURANI eau de toilette by
Mariella Burani. Euro wCosmetics. Funo, Italy.
Double opaque roses serve as a stopper. 4.5ml
(.17oz.).

PARCE QUE parfum by Parfums Capucci. Paris, France. "FRANCE" appears on the bottom of the 1.87ml (1/16oz.) bottle. The fragrance was introduced in 1963.

BOUQUET perfume by Cardinal. NY, NY. The 3.75ml (1/8oz.) bottle from the 1930s has a white cap with a blue stone in the center.

GARDENIA perfume by Cardinal. NY, NY. 10ml (1/3oz.) The bottle is from the 1930s.

CARDIN parfum by fashion designer Pierre Cardin. Paris, France. The 3.75ml (1/8oz.) bottle was designed by Pierre Dinand.

Right: ORIENT perfume by Cardinal. NY, NY.
3.75ml (1/8oz.).

CARNEGIE PINK perfume by Hattie Carnegie.
NY, NY. 1.87ml (1/16oz.).

POPPY MUSK perfume by Carme Internaltional. Inc.
6ml (1/5oz.).

BELLODGIA extrait by Parfums Caron. Paris, France.
Parfums Caron was founded by Ernest Daltroff in 1903.
The 7.5ml (1/4oz.) bottle is marked "CARON" and
"FRANCE" on the bottom of the bottle.

FLEUR DE ROCAILLE parfum by Parfums Caron. Paris, France. 1.87ml (1/16oz.).

FLEUR DE ROCAILLE eau de toilette by Parfums Caron. Paris, France. The 3ml (.1oz.) miniature is a replica of the classic original bottle design of Michel Morsetti. The floral fragrance was introduced in 1933.

BELLODGIA parfum by Parfums Caron. Paris, France. The floral fragrance, named for an island in Italy, was introduced in 1927. The 15ml (1/2oz.) bottle was designed by Felicie Vanpouille.

LA NUIT DE NOEL ("Christmas Eve") parfum by Parfums Caron. Paris, France. The oriental fragrance was introduced in 1922. "CARON" is molded into the back of the bottle. 3.75ml (1/8oz.).

Left: FRENCH CANCAN parfum by Parfums Caron. Paris, France. The 7.5ml (1/4oz.) bottle has a long glass stopper. The fragrance was introduced in 1936.

MUGUET DU BONHEUR eau de cologne by Parfums Caron. Paris, France. 3.75ml (1/8oz.). The fragrance was introduced in 1952.

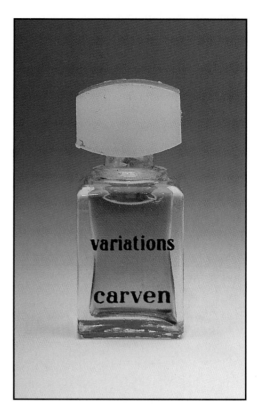

VARIATIONS parfum by Parfums Carven. Paris, France. 1.87ml (1/16oz.).

MA GRIFFE parfum by Parfums Carven. Paris, France. The 1.87ml (1/16oz.) black-lettered bottle has "SGD" (the trademark for Saint Gobain Desjonqueres) on the bottom . The chypre-floral fragrance was introduced in 1946.

MA GRIFFE ("My Signature") parfum de toilette by Parfums Carven. Paris, France. Parfums Carven was established in 1944 by Maurice Pinot, Georges Baud, and Jean Prodhon. They named their business after a good friend, Madame Carven. 5ml (.17oz.).

MADAME DE CARVEN eau de toilette by Parfums Carven. Paris, France. 5ml (.16oz.) The fragrance was introduced in 1979.

Left: BREATHLESS essence by Charbert. NY, NY. Charbert Perfumes was established in 1933, the same year this fragrance was introduced. "CHARBERT" is molded into the bottom of the 7.5ml (1/4oz.) bottle.

CREDO parfum by Pridu Cebehrsk. La Parfum CREDO is contained in a 7.5ml (1/4oz.) bottle.

SPICE perfume by Champrel, NY, NY. The 7.5ml (1/4oz.) bottle is from the 1940s.

NINO CERRUTI eau de parfum pour femme by Parfums Nino Cerrutti. Paris, France. The 3.7ml (1/8oz.) black signature bottle has a black needle stopper.

CHANEL NO 5 eau de parfum by Chanel. Paris, France. The 4ml (.13oz.) bottle with a glass stopper has the "SGD" trademark on the bottom. The floral-aldehyde fragrance was a favorite of Marilyn Monroe.

CHANEL NO 5 parfum by Chanel. Paris, France. Gabrielle Chanel founded her couture house in 1910. She introduced "CHANEL NO 5" in 1921. The glass bottle with a glass dauber has "CHANEL" molded into the bottom. 7.5ml (1/4oz.).

COCO parfum by Chanel. Paris, France. 1.87ml (1/16oz.) The bottle is by Saint Gobain Desjonqueres, marked "SGD," and has a glass stopper. The floral-oriental fragrance was introduced in 1984 to honor Gabrielle "Coco" Chanel.

PAMYR parfum by
Charles V. Paris, France.
3.75ml (1/8oz.).

1800 parfum by Charles
V. Paris, France. 1.87ml
(1/16oz.).

CROYANCE parfum
by Charles V. Paris,
France. The 7.5ml
(1/4oz.) bottle is from
the 1950s.

CORDON D'OR parfum
by Charles V. Paris, France.
3.75ml (1/8oz.).

SENCHAL perfume by Charles of the Ritz Group Ltd. NY, NY. 3.75ml (1/8oz.) Charles Jundt opened a beauty salon in the Ritz-Carlton Hotel in 1916 and introduced perfumes in 1927 — hence "Charles of the Ritz."

HANADE parfum by Chaurand. Paris, France. 1.87ml (1/16oz.).

Right: APRIL SHOWERS eau de cologne by Cheramy. Paris, France. Founded by Raymond Couin in 1921, Cheramy was sold and became a subsidiary company of Houbigant in 1922. Cheramy introduced low-priced perfumes. APRIL SHOW-ERS was introduced in 1921. The 15ml (1/2oz.) bottle by Verreries Brosse is from the 1920s.

IRIS DE SENTEUS parfum by Cheramy. Paris, France. The 3.75ml (1/8oz.) bottle is from the 1920s.

OH LA LA parfum by Parfums Ciro. Paris, France. Ciro was established in 1932. The 1.87ml (1/16oz.) bottle has "FRANCE HP" molded into the bottom of the bottle. The fragrance was introduced in 1959.

SURRENDER parfum by Parfums Ciro. Paris, France. The 3ml (.1oz.) bottle is by Wheaton Glass. A circled "W" is on the bottom of the bottle. The fragrance was introduced in 1932.

CHESS PIECES by Mary Chess. NY, NY. Mary Chess founded her perfumery in 1932 and introduced CHESS PIECES in 1938. The 3/4 dram 3ml (3/32oz.) bottles are about 75mm and have Bakelite tops. The King holds GARDENIA. The Bishop holds STRATEGY. The Rook holds WHITE LILAC. The Knight is unmarked.

GRAND AMOUR parfum by L. Clavel. Paris, France. 1.87ml (1/16oz.).

STRATEGY toilette water by Mary Chess. NY, NY. STRATEGY was introduced in 1942. The 7.5ml (1/4oz.) squared glass bottle is from the late 1940s. Note the gold paper box with chess board squares and chess pieces.

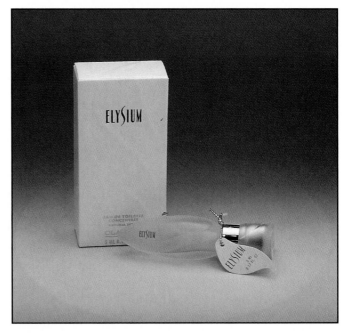

VIVID parfum by Liz Claiborne Cosmetics, Inc. NY, NY. This floral fragrance was introduced in 1993. The cobalt blue bottle holds 3ml (1/8oz.).

ELYSIUM eau de toilette natural spray by Clarins. Neuilly, France. The beautiful frosted glass bottle holds 5ml (.17oz.) of the floral-fruity fragrance, created by Clarins "to stir the senses." Described as "Blissful, delightful," from 1959. On the box it states: "Sometimes the heart see's what the eye cannot," with the letters "JCC."

FLORIENT and FLORIENT flowers of the orient by Colgate & Co. Jersey City, NJ. The 1.87ml (1/16oz.) bottles are from the teens. The fragrances were introduced in 1912.

LILY OF THE VALLEY perfume by Colgate & Co. The company was foundd by William Colgate in 1906, introducing French-style perfumes in 1920. Jersey City, NJ. A 3.75ml (1/8 oz.) bottle in a metal jacket from the 1920s.

NINJA parfum by Parfums de Coeur. Paris, France. 7.5ml (1/4oz.).

LILY OF THE VALLEY perfume by Colgate Palmolive-Peet Co., which was formed in a 1928 merger. Jersey City, NJ. 5.6ml (3/16oz.).

VIOLET WATER by Colgate & Co. Jersey City, NJ. 3.75ml (1 dram, or 1/8oz.) The brass-capped bottle was made between 1910 and 1920.

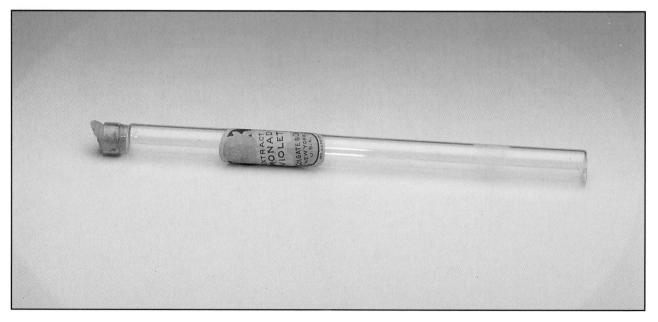

MONAD VIOLET by Colgate & Co. Jersey City, NJ. The 3.75ml (1 dram, or 1/8oz.) vial holds a scent created by William Colgate in 1901.

FAME parfum by
Parfums Corday
Inc. NY, NY.
1.87ml (1/16oz.)
The fragrance was
introduced in 1946.

TOUJOURS MOI
parfum by Parfums
Corday Inc. Paris,
France. Corday was
founded by Blanche
Arvoy in 1924. 3.5ml
(.12oz.).

POSSESSION de Corday by Parfums Corday Inc. NY, NY. Perfume
made in France. The fragrance, contained in a bottle with a brown and
gold label, sits in a clear plastic case. Introduced in 1939. 3ml (1/10oz.).

PRESTIGE perfume by Congoleum Corp. Kearny,
NJ. 7.5ml (1/4oz.).

EMERAUDE parfum by Coty, Inc. Paris, France. Coty was established in 1900. The classic frosted glass bottle with a brass stopper cover has "EMERAUDE" embossed on the glass. 7.5ml (1/4oz.)

TOUJOURS MOI parfum by Parfums Corday Inc. Paris, France. The 7.5ml (1/4oz.) classic bottle has the "CP" seal and the bottom of the bottle has "HP" molded into the glass. An oriental fragrance introduced in 1923.7/12

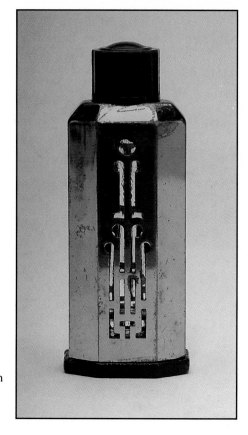

EMERAUDE parfum by Coty, Inc. Paris, France. The 3.75ml (1/8oz.) hexagon glass bottle is encased in brass, sits on a green base, and has a green cap. EMERAUDE was introduced in 1923.

L'AIMANT eau de toilette by Coty, Inc. Paris, France. "COTY" is molded into the bottom of the bottle. 20ml (.65oz.) L'AIMANT was introduced in 1927, and this bottle dates from the late 1920s.

L'AIMANT parfum by Coty, Inc. Paris, France. The 7.5ml (1/4oz.) gold-lettered bottle has the "HP" trademark, and a "C" on the octagon shaped cap.

EMERAUDE and L'AIMANT parfum de toilette by Coty Division of Pfizer. NY, NY. The two fragrances are shown in their modern 15ml (1/2oz.) bottles with gold crown caps.

MUSE perfume de Coty by Coty, Inc. NY, NY. The 1.87ml (1/16oz.) bottle has a gold label.

MUGUET DES BOIS perfume by Coty, Inc. NY, NY. A pale green fragrance in a 3.69ml (1/8oz.) clear glass bottle with a blue stopper.

PARIS perfume by Coty, Inc. NY, NY. The 4ml (.13oz.) bottle is encased in a gold metal sleeve with a blue base and a gold cap. PARIS was introduced in 1921.

L'EFFLEUR perfume by Coty, Inc. NY, NY. 3.69ml (1/8oz.)

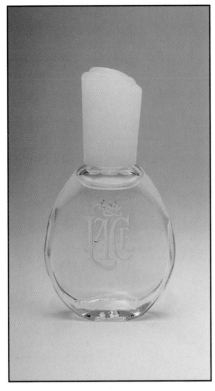

TRULY LACE perfume by Coty, Inc. NY, NY. The 3.69ml (1/8oz.) bottle has gold lettering and an opaque plastic stopper.

STYX parfum by Coty, Inc. Paris, France. The classic 7.5ml (1/4oz.) bottle has "COTY FRANCE" molded into the bottom and a frosted glass stopper. The label is embossed. STYX was introduced in 1912.

IMPREVU perfume by Coty, Inc. NY, NY. The 1.87ml (1/16oz.) bottle by Pochet et du Courval has gold lettering.

IMPREVU perfume by Coty Division of Pfizer. NY, NY. 3.75ml (1/8oz.) IMPREVU was introduced in 1965.

MASUMI perfume by Coty Division of Pfizer. NY, NY. The 3.75ml (1/8oz.) bottle comes in a black plastic box. The fragrance was introduced in 1965.

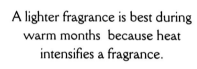

A lighter fragrance is best during warm months because heat intensifies a fragrance.

Coty bottle. A Rene Lalique design from 1914. The bottle was used for LIPAS POURPRE and other scents. 7.5ml (1/4oz.)

Coty bottles measuring 6ml (.20oz.), 9ml (.30oz.), and 12ml (.40oz.), with "COTY" molded into the bottom.

SPARKLING GOLD toilette water by Daggett & Ramsdell. Established in 1890 in Newark, NJ. The company introduced perfumes in 1937. SPARKLING GOLD was introduced in 1952 and distributed by The Fuller Brush Co. of Hartford, CT. The 3.75ml (1 dram, or 1/8oz.) bottle is from the 1950s.

PAILLETTES eau de toilette by Enrico Coveri. Euroitalia of Milan Italy. The 6ml (.21oz.) frosted glass bottle has a red stopper.

EMPREINTE parfum de Courreges. Paris, France. The gold-lettered, gold-capped bottle holds a chypre-floral animalic fragrance introduced by Andre Courreges in 1970. 3.75ml (1/8oz.)

LAGUNA eau de toilette by Parfums Salvador Dali. Paris, France. A flacon miniature reproduction. The clear glass Dali bottle has a green colored floral-fresh fragrance, introduced in 1991. 5ml (.17oz.). Salvador Dali was a Surrealistic painter from Spain.

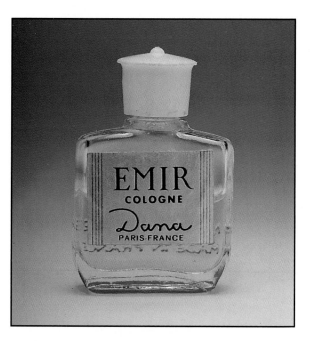

EMIR cologne by Dana Parfums Corp. Paris, France. NY, NY. "NOT FOR SALE, MADE IN FRANCE" is molded into the back of the 3ml (.1oz.) bottle. "DANA" is molded into the bottom of the bottle. EMIR was introduced in 1936.

TABU parfum by Dana Parfums Corp. Established by Javier Serra in 1932 in Paris, France. 1.87ml (1/16oz.) "HP" appears on the bottom of the bottle. The fragrance was introduced in 1932.

TABU by Dana Parfums Corp. Paris, France. The metal tube contains lipstick on one end with a 1.87ml (1/16oz.) glass perfume bottle inside the tube cover.

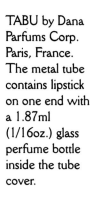

OMNI perfume by Deborah International Beauty Ltd. NY, NY. 15ml (1/2oz.).

LYRA eau de toilette by Parfums Alain Delon. Paris, France and Geneva, Switzerland. The 5ml (.17oz.) bottle contains a floral-ambery fragrance.

CHYPRE perfume by Deltah Perfumes, Inc. NY, NY. 15ml (1/2oz.).

RENDEZVOUS perfume by Deltah Perfumes, Inc. NY, NY. 7.5ml (1/4oz.).

JASMIN perfume by De Marsay, Inc. U.S.A. The 3ml (.1oz.) bottle is from the 1930s.

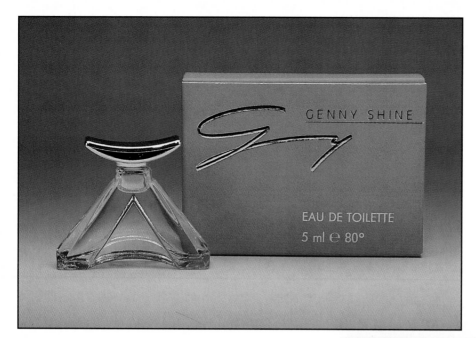

GENNY SHINE eau de toilette by Diana de Silva Cosmetics. Milan, Italy. The floral-fruity fragrance was introduced in 1993 and is contained in a 5ml (.16oz.) bottle.

HOPE and INTERLUDE parfums by Frances Denney. Philadelphia, PA. HOPE was introduced in 1952, INTERLUDE in 1962. 1.87ml (1/16oz.)

LES COPAINS eau de toilette by Diana de Silva Cosmetics. Milan, Italy. The 5ml (1/6oz.) bottle has black lettering and a black cap.

MISS DIOR eau de toilette by Parfums Christian Dior. Established in Paris, France in 1946. The 5ml (.17oz.) bottle is a beautiful replica of the original 1947 creation. The chypre-floral animalic fragrance was introduced in 1947.

TENDRE POISON parfum by Christian Dior Perfumes, Inc. Distributed from NY, NY. The green glass bottle has "HP" on the bottom. A floral-fresh fragrance, introduced in 1994. 5ml (.17oz.).

DIORESSENCE bath perfume concentrate pour le bain by Parfums Christian Dior. Paris, France. An oriental-spicy fragrance introduced in 1980 and contained in a 7.5ml (1/4oz.) bottle.

DIVINE perfume by D'Orsay. Paris, France. The familiar D'Orsay bottle contains a perfume introduced in 1947. 5ml (1/6oz.).

CHARMANTE perfume by Parfum D'or de Paris, Ltd. Paris, France. 15ml (1/2oz.).

INTOXICATION perfume by D'Orsay. Paris, France. NY, NY. The fragrance was introduced in 1942. 3.75ml (1/8oz.)

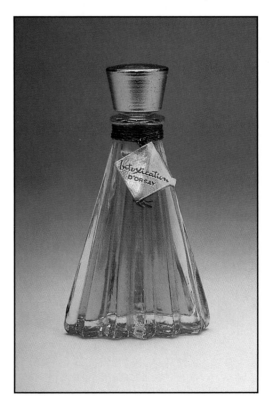

INTOXICATION perfume by D'Orsay. Paris, France. NY, NY. A 3.75ml (1/8oz.) fluted glass bottle.

VOULEZ-VOUS parfum by D'Orsay. Paris, France. "D'ORSAY" is molded into the bottom of the 1.87ml (1/16oz.) bottle.

GARDENIA perfume by Duchess of Paris. Jersey City, NJ. 3.75ml (1/8oz.) The brass-capped bottle is from the 1940s.

A Bakelite-cased glass bottle by DuBe. NY, NY. The string probably held the fragrance name. The 7.5ml (2 drams, or 1/4oz.) bottle dates from the 1940s.

INFATLUT 07 perfume by Duchess of Paris. NY, NY. The milk glass bottle holds 3.75ml (1/8oz.).

SINGAPORE NIGHTS perfume was introduced by Duchess of Paris in 1934. NY, NY. 3.75ml (1/8oz.).

NAUGHTY perfume by Duchess of Paris, a subsidiary company of Jolind, Inc. NY, NY. 3.75ml (1/8oz.). The fragrance was introduced in 1937.

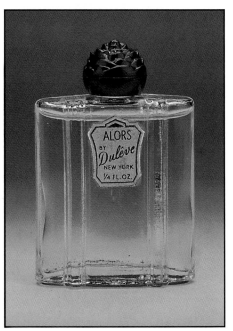

ALORS perfume by Duleve. NY, NY. The 7.5ml (1/4oz.) bottle is from the 1930s, and has a green flower bulb cap.

Duchess of Paris bottles used by the company for different inexpensive fragrances.

LILAC by Duvinne. The bottle is from the 1920s and holds 5ml (1/6oz.).

360 parfum by Perry Ellis. Distributed by Sanofi Beaute, Inc. NY, NY. Manufactured by Parfums Stern. Paris, France. The floral fragrance, created in 1993, is contained in a 4ml (1/8oz.) bottle.

DOLCE & GABBANA eau de toilette by Euroitalia. Monza, Italy. The floral-oriental fragrance was introduced in 1993 by Italian designers Domenico Dolce and Stefano Gabbana. The 5ml (.16oz.) clear glass bottle, with a red stopper, comes in a red velvet finished box.

GOLDEN SHADOWS perfume by Parfums Evyan. Evyan was founded in 1930 by Baron Walter Langer Von Langendorff and his wife Lady Evyan. The fragrance was introduced in 1950. The hexagon bottle has a flower-topped cap. 5ml (1/6oz.).

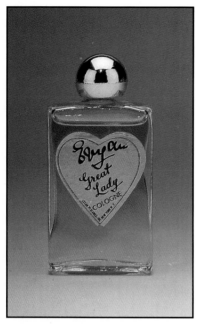

GREAT LADY cologne by Parfums Evyan. NY, NY. The 7.5ml (1/4oz.) square bottle has a heart-shaped label made of gold paper. The fragrance was introduced in 1957.

WHITE SHOULDERS perfume by Parfums Evyan. NY, NY. WHITE SHOULDERS was introduced in 1943. It is said that the name was chosen after a dinner party, where a compliment was paid to Lady Evyan's lovely white shoulders. The 7.5ml (1/4oz.) bottle was made in Italy, and has a gold embossed label.

WHITE SHOULDERS cologne by Parfums Evyan. NY, NY. A 7.5ml (1/4oz.) heart-shaped bottle. The back of the label reads "Not for sale, compliments of Evyan." WHITE SHOULDERS was Evyan's best seller.

WHITE SHOULDERS cologne by Parfums Evyan. NY, NY. The 3.75ml (1/8oz.) bottle from the 1950s has a pink label and pink cap. The pink heart-shaped pillow has a cologne vial with a plastic dauber that attaches to the pillow. The reverse side has a gold heart-shaped paper label.

FABERGE perfume sample by Faberge, Inc. NY, NY. From 1960. "The Higbee Co. Cleveland, OH" is stamped on the paper. The tiny vial has a gold stopper and is attached to the paper flambeau. "You're playing with fire with FABERGE" is printed on the paper flambeau.

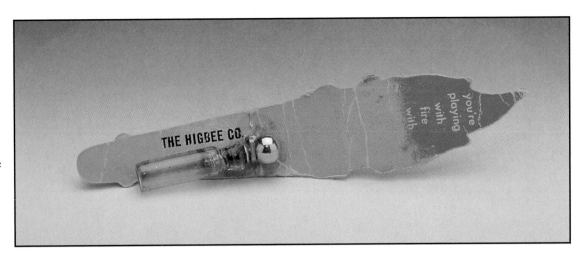

WHITE SHOULDERS perfume by Parfums Evyan. The 5ml (1/6oz.) hexagon bottle sits in a gold metal base with a dull brass sleeve covering. The 5ml (1/6oz.) round bottle with gold lettering has WHITE SHOULDERS on the base and a bright brass sleeve covering.

FLAMBEAU cologne by Faberge, Inc. NY, NY. FLAMBEAU was introduced in 1955. "FABERGE" is molded into the bottom of the 15ml (1/2oz.) bottle.

ELLIPSE parfum by Jacques Fath Parfums. Paris, France. The green bottle holds 3.5ml (1/8oz.).

EXPRESSION parfum by Jacques Fath Parfums. Paris, France. The floral-chypre ambery fragrance was introduced in 1977. "JF" and a circled "R" is molded into the bottom of the 3.75ml (1/8oz.) bottle.

ASJA eau de parfum by Fendi. Parma, Italy. 5ml (.17oz.) The black bottle with a red cap holds a floral-oriental fragrance, introduced in 1993.

FATH DE FATH eau de toilette by Jacques Fath Parfums. Bois and Paris, France. A floral-fruity fragrance is contained in this 3.5ml (1/8oz.) faceted bottle, which has no markings.

FEMINA eau de parfum by Alberta Ferretti. Milan, Italy. A green glass 7.5ml (1/4oz.) bottle with an opaque pink spiraling stopper.

FINESSE cologne by Finesse, Inc. Chicago, IL. 15ml (1/2oz.).

BAHAMOUR De Fontenay. Paris, France. The 30ml (1oz.) glass bottle has "MADE IN FRANCE" on the bottom and a frosted stopper.

PETAL MIST perfume by Forcelli Co. Bohemia, NY. 3/5ml (1/8oz.). Introduced in 1994.

MING TOY parfum, introduced in 1923 by Forest Parfumery. Founded by Leon Cohn in Paris, France in 1910. The 7.5ml (1/4oz.) glass stoppered bottle has "HP" and "MADE IN FRANCE" molded into the bottom.

APPLE BLOSSOM toilette water by The Fuller Brush Co. Hartford, CT. The 3.75ml (1 dram, or 1/8oz.) bottle is from the 1950s.

LEADING LADY toilette water by The Fuller Brush Co. Hartford, CT. Introduced in 1956. 3.75ml (1/8oz.).

BOURRASQUE perfume by Le Galion. Paris, France. Prince Murat founded the perfumery. BOURRASQUE was introduced in 1937. The 1ml (1/32oz.) bottle has a gold foil label and a brass cap. A galleon is stamped into the brass cap and "LE GALION" is molded into the bottom of the bottle.

JASMINE parfum de toilette by Le Galion. Paris, France. 7.5ml (1/4oz.) JASMINE was introduced in 1937. "L.G." is on the bottom of the bottle and a galleon is engraved on the cap.

JEAN-PAUL GAULTIER parfum by Parfums Jean-Paul Gaultier (a French designer) and Beauty Prestige International. Paris, France. The torso bottle holds 3.5ml (.1oz.) and is covered in a frosted corset. The bottle is contained in a grey plastic can. The floral-fruity fragrance was introduced in 1993.

LITTLE GREEN APPLE eau de parfum by Giftique, Division of New York Pencil Co., Inc. Long Island City, NY. The 14.21ml (1/2oz.) bottle from the 1980s has "ITALY" molded into the bottom.

DONNA eau de toilette by Parfums Gherardini. Firenza, Italy. A "G" is molded into the front of the bottle. "GHERARDINI FIRENZA" is molded into the bottom of the 6ml (1/5oz.) bottle.

Right: EAU DE CHARLOTTE eau de toilette by Annick Goutal. Paris, France. The 8ml (.26oz.) bottle contains a floral-fruity fragrance introduced in 1986.

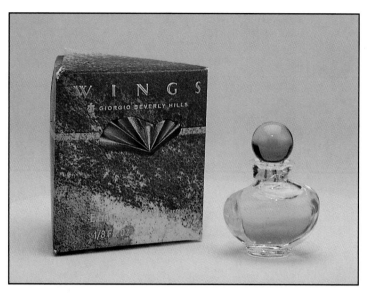

WINGS Extraordinary Perfume by Giorgio Beverly Hills. Beverly Hills, CA. 3.5ml (1/8oz.) The bottle holds a floral-oriental fragrance introduced in 1992 and is topped with a sky blue stopper.

GARDENIA PASSION eau de toilette by Annick Goutal. Paris, France. The fragrance is pure gardenia, introduced in 1990. 8ml (.26oz.).

CHALEUR perfume by Grafton Products Corp. Norwalk, CT. Blended with imported oils in the U.S.A. 15ml (1/2oz.)

CABOCHARD eau de parfum by Parfums Gres. Paris, France. The 3.2ml (.1oz.) bottle neck has a bow and a frosted stopper with a "G." "BOTTLE MADE IN FRANCE" is molded into the bottom. A chypre-floral animalic fragrance, originally introduced in 1959 and reintroduced in 1972.

CABOCHARD parfum by Parfums Gres. Paris, France. Gres Couture was founded by Germaine Barton in 1930. Mme. Alix Gres introduced CABOCHARD. 1.87ml (1/16oz.).

CABOTINE de Gres eau de parfum by Parfums Gres. Paris, France. The 3.2ml (.1oz.) bottle contains a floral-green fragrance introduced in 1990. The bottle has a band of opaque, emerald green flowers and a cluster of emerald flowers as a stopper. "BOTTLE MADE IN FRANCE" is on the bottom.

CHAMADE parfum by Guerlain Parfums. Paris, France. A classic French perfume, "Feminine Assured," CHAMADE was created by Jean-Paul Guerlain in 1969. A floral semi-oriental fragrance. 1.87ml (1/16oz.)

CHAMADE parfum by Guerlain Parfums. Paris, France. The 5ml (1/6oz.) bottle represents an upside-down heart. The stopper has "CHAMADE" in gold letters and the bottle has "MADE IN FRANCE" molded into the bottom. The 15ml (1/2oz.) bottle has "GUERLAIN" in gold letters on the base and the reverse side has "1/2 OZ" in gold letters on the base.

IMPERIALE eau de cologne by Guerlain Parfums. Established in 1828 by Pierre-Francois-Pascal Guerlain in Paris, France. He created IMPERIALE for the Empress Eugenie in 1853. The reintroduction in 1983 is a "modele d'essai," meaning an attempt to recreate the original design. 7.5ml (1/4oz.)

JARDINS DE BAGATELLE eau de toilette by Guerlain Parfums. Paris, France. The floral fragrance by Jean-Paul Guerlain was introduced in 1983. A "modele d'essai" 7.5ml (1/4oz.) bottle with "HP" molded into the bottom. The fragrance was named for Queen Marie Antoinette's retreat.

L'HEURE BLEUE parfum by Guerlain Parfums. Paris, France. L'HEURE BLEUE ("Blue Hour") was conceived by Jacques Guerlain in 1912. A floral-ambery fragrance. The 2ml (.17oz.) bottle is a "modele d'essai" with a copy of the original presentation box. "HP" is molded into the bottom of the bottle. The original bottle was created by Baccarat.

PARURE eau de toilette by Guerlain Parfums. Paris, France. PARURE, French for adornment, is a chypre-floral animalic fragrance by Jean-Paul Guerlain, created in 1975. 3.75ml (1/8oz.).

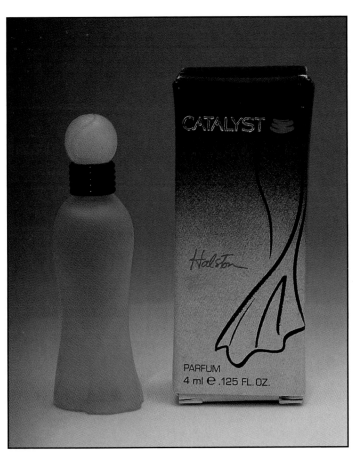

CATALYST parfum by Halston Fragrances. NY, NY. The floral fragrance, introduced in 1993, is contained in a 4ml (.125oz.) bottle.

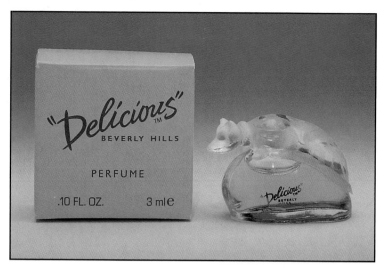

TOUCH perfume by Fred Hayman, Beverly Hills. Beverly Hills, CA. The 3.7ml (1/8oz.) bottle has the Fred Hayman monogram in gold.

DELICIOUS perfume by Gale Hayman Inc. Beverly Hills, CA. A floral fragrance introduced in 1993. The 3ml (.1oz.) bottle is the same leopard design as is used for BEVERLY HILLS glamour perfume.

ROYAL PURPLE toilette water by The Herb Farm Shop Ltd. Elizabeth, NJ. Compounded from the English formula in the U.S.A. Distributed from NY, NY. The 10ml (2.75 drams, or 1/3oz.) bottle is from the 1940s.

PARFUM D'HERMES eau de toilette by Parfum Hermes. Paris, France and Milan, Italy. The oval bottle has gold lettering. 5ml (1/6oz.). A semi-oriental fragrance introduced in 1984.

RED CARNATION by
Hess. Rochester, NY.
By The Youthful Tint
Manufacturing Co.
7.5ml (1/4oz.). The
vial-type bottle has a
brass cap and is from
the 1920s.

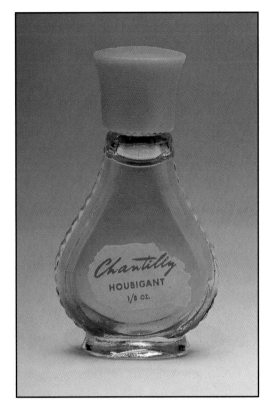

CHANTILLY parfum
by Houbigant. Paris,
France. The classic
French blend was
created by Paul
Parquet in 1941. An
oriental-ambery
fragrance. The
3.75ml (1/8oz.) bottle
is from the 1940s.

INDIAN SUMMER cologne by
Houbigant. NY, NY. Paris, France.
Houbigant Perfumes was founded by
Jean-Francois Houbigant in 1774. The
beautiful bottle is covered in autumn
leaves. 15ml (1/2oz.).

LE PARFUM IDEAL
perfume by
Houbigant. Paris,
France. 7.5ml (1/4oz.).
The bottle has a gold
foil label with "N3KO"
printed on the back.
The bottle has
"HOUBIGANT,
FRANCE" molded
into the bottom. LE
PARFUM IDEAL was
introduced in 1900.
The bottle fits into the
brass case with a
hinged top.
"HOUBIGANT" is
molded into the case
bottom.

QUELQUES FLEURS perfume by Houbigant. Paris, France. A 3.75ml (1/8oz.) bottle with a brass cap.

QUELQUES FLEURS perfume by Houbigant. Paris, France. 15ml (1/2oz.) This is the first multi-floral fragrance, created in 1912 by Robert Bienaime. The beautiful bottle from the early 1920s has gold leaf covering its stopper.

FLAME by Hove. Novelle Orleans. New Orleans, LA. 1.87ml (1/16oz.). The Wheaton bottle is from the 1950s. The circled "W" is molded into the bottom of the bottle.

BOUQUET SUPREME by Federici. Distributed by Howe Co. Inc. Seattle, WA. The 3.75ml (1/8oz.) glass bottle has a white cap with a gemstone attached. The bottle is from the 1940s.

GARDENIA by Hollywood. Distributed by Howe Co. Inc. Seattle, WA. and NY, NY. The 3.75ml (1/8oz.) bottle is from the 1940s.

HOYT perfumer by Hoyt Co. Inc. Perfumers. Memphis, TN. A 7.5ml (1/4oz.) glass purse flacon. "HOYT PERFUMER" is stamped into the black brass cap.

HOYT'S cologne, The Original 1868, by Hoyt Co. Inc. Perfumers. Memphis, TN. Distributed from NY, NY. "HOYT CO. INC. PERFUMERS, MEMPHIS" is molded into the back of the bottle. The 7.5ml (1/4oz.) bottle is from the 1950s.

STAMBOUL by Hoyt Co. Inc. Perfumers. Memphis, TN. Distributed from NY, NY. "HOYT'S" is molded into the bottom of the 7.5ml (1/4oz.) bottle.

GEMEY perfume by
Richard Hudnut. NY, NY.
The firm was established
in 1880. The firm was
active from the 1800s into
the 1950s. The fragrance
was introduced in 1923.
The 3.75ml (1/8oz.) bottle
is from the 1920s.

YANKY CLOVER toilette
water by Richard Hudnut.
NY, NY. Rivera Sales Co.,
authorized distributors.
"NY, NY." is printed on
the label. The fragrance
was introduced in 1944.
3.75ml (1/8oz.).

Richard Hudnut used this .5 dram bottle for his
fragrances in the 1920s. The bottle is frosted glass
with a metal post and cork stopper.

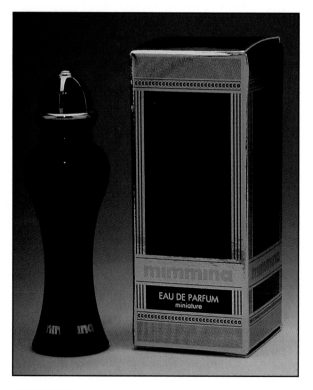

MIMMINA eau de parfum by Intercosma West. Italy.
The 5ml (.17oz.) bottle is cobalt blue, and the stopper
is crowned in blue and gold. "MIMMINA" appears on
the bottle in gold lettering.

IRRESISTIBLE perfume by Irresistible Distributor. NY, NY. The bottle, with a red cap, has "BOTTLE MADE IN USA" molded into the bottom. The 6ml (1/5oz.) bottle is from the 1940s.

IRRESISTIBLE perfume by Irresistible Distributor. NY, NY. The fragrance was introduced in 1932. The 5ml (1/6oz.) bottle is from the 1940s.

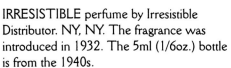

Above: FORGET ME NOT eau de parfum by Parfums Jamaica. Kingston, Jamaica. West Indies. 7.5ml (1/4oz.).

Left: SOURIRE FLEURI perfume by Isabey. Paris, France. Established in 1924 by Maurice Loewe, the perfumery was known for high-quality perfumes and was most active during the 1920s and 1930s. This fragrance was introduced in 1926. The bottle, from the late 1920s, has a brass cap. 7.5ml (1/4oz.).

JEUNESSE eau de parfum by Parfums Jamaica. Kingston, Jamaica. West Indies. 15ml (1/2oz.).

BEN HUR perfume by Jergens. A company founded by Andrew Jergens in Cincinnati, OH. The blown glass bottle has gold around the neck. 3.75ml (1/8oz.).

BEN HUR perfume, introduced in 1904 by Jergens. Cincinnati, OH. 3ml (.1oz.).

BEN HUR perfume by Jergens. Cincinnati, OH. 7.5ml (1/4oz.) The 1930s bottle is from Carr Lowry Glass Co.

BEN HUR perfume by Jergens. Cincinnati, OH. The 7.5ml (1/4oz.) bottle is an example of their later bottles and labels. The Carr-Lowry trademark "CL" is molded into the bottom of the bottle.

GARDENIA eau de cologne by Jergens. Cincinnati, OH. 15ml (1/2oz.). "JERGENS" is molded into the bottom of the bottle.

GARDENIA perfume by Jolind, Inc. NY, NY. A division of Joubert. The 3ml (.1oz.) bottle is from the 1930s.

JOOP! BERLIN eau de toilette by Parfums Joop! Paris, France and Hamburg, Germany. The modern bottle has a sun-yellow cap and box. 5ml (.17oz.).

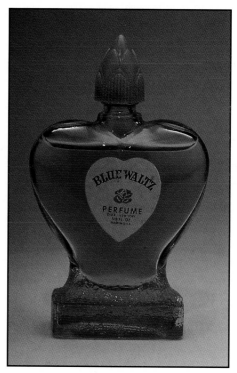

JOOP! NUIT D'ETE eau de toilette by Parfums Joop! Paris, France and Hamburg, Germany. 5ml (.17oz.) Summer Night. A hint of heaven between twilight and dawn. An oriental fragrance.

BLUE WALTZ perfume by Joubert. NY, NY. 18.75ml (5/8oz.) The classic BLUE WALTZ bottle has "MADE IN USA" molded into the bottom. The fragrance was introduced in 1927. The bottle is from the 1940s.

BLUE WALTZ perfume by Joubert. NY, NY. Distributed from Jersey City, NJ. The 7.5ml (1/4oz.) bottle is from the 1930s, and features a glass dauber attached to the blue Bakelite cap.

TRES JOURDAN eau de parfum by Parfums Charles Jourdan. Paris, France. 5ml (.17oz.).

SCULPTURA perfume by Jovan Inc. Chicago, IL. The 3.75ml (1/8oz.) square bottle of black glass has a sleek silver woman's torso as a stopper cap.

WOMENSWEAR BY ALEXANDER JULIAN fine perfume by Alexander Julian. Distributed by Paul Sebastian Inc. Ocean, NJ. 7.5ml (1/4oz.). The sanded, sea green, glass jar bottle contains a floral fragrance, sealed with a orchid cap. The fragrance was introduced in 1992.

KASHAYA eau de toilette de Kenzo. Paris, France. Distributed by Tamaras. 5ml (.17oz.).

NOA NOA eau de toilette by Otto Kern and Beautycos Cosmetics. Frankfurt, Germany; Paris, France and London England. 5ml (.17oz.). A leaf drapes over the shoulder of the bottle.

BLAZER cologne by Anne Klein. Distributed by Helena Rubinstein Inc. NY, NY. A 15ml (1/2oz.) bottle.

C K ONE. A unisex fragrance introduced in 1994 by Calvin Klein Cosmetics Corp. NY, NY. A 1.87ml (1/16oz.) vial.

CALVIN KLEIN cologne by Calvin Klein Cosmetics Corp. NY, NY. 7.5ml (1/4oz.).

ETERNITY perfume by Calvin Klein Cosmetics Corp. NY, NY. 4ml (.13oz.). The floral-fresh fragrance was introduced in 1988. The classic bottle has a silver stopper.

PASCALLE perfume pulsette by Kensington Inc. Greensboro, NC. 7.5ml (1/4oz.).

LAVENDER SALTS by Keystone Perfume Co. Philadelphia, PA. 7.5ml (1/4oz.). The early 1900s bottle has a department store label on the reverse side.

C'EST LA VIE! eau de parfum by Christian Lacroix. Paris, France. 4ml (.13oz.). The floral-ambery fragrance was introduced in 1986. The pendant bottle, with a cord, was designed by Maurice Roger.

AMBRE, IRISE, and VERT parfum by Bernard Lalande. Paris, France. A group of 1.87ml (1/16oz.) bottles with the "SGD" trademark molded into the bottom of each.

LALIQUE eau de toilette by Lalique Parfums. Paris, France. 4.5ml (.15oz.) A floral fragrance introduced in 1992 by Marie-Claude Lalique, of course, in a Lalique bottle — the "Honeysuckle Flacon."

Right: LANCETTI ELLE eau de toilette by Lancetti and S.B.P. Milan, Italy. 5ml (.17oz.). The leaf-draped bottle has a leaf stopper.

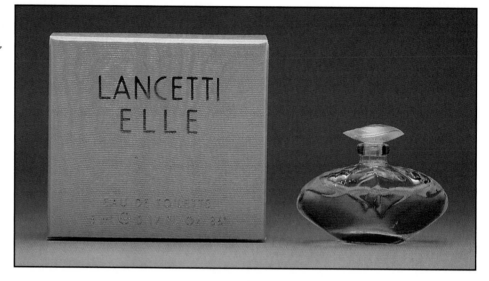

Apply fragrances to the pulse points — wrists, inner elbows, throat and neck areas — for a lasting effect.

MAGIE parfum by Parfums Lancome. Paris, France. The 3.75ml (1/8oz.) bottle is a rectangular block of crystal twisted as if by magic — actually, by Baccarat. The original design was by Sophie Frydlender for Lancome. The fragrance was introduced in 1949. "LANCOME, MADE IN FRANCE" is molded into the bottom of the bottle.

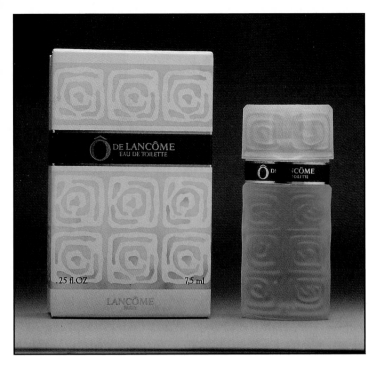

O DE LANCOME eau de toilette by Parfums Lancome. Lancome was established in 1935 by Armand Petitjean in Paris, France. The frosted glass bottle holds a chypre fragrance. 7.5ml (1/4oz.).

SIKKIM parfum by Parfums Lancome. Paris, France. 3.5ml (1/8oz.).

APPLE BLOSSOM perfume by Lander Co., Inc. The Lander Co. was established in 1920 by Charles H. Oestreich in NY, NY. 7.5ml (1/4oz.). A 25-cent sticker is on the bottom of the bottle from the late 1940s.

PINK PETALS perfume by Lander Co., Inc. NY, NY. The bottle is 3.75ml (1/8oz.). The label states 1/4oz., but is obviously incorrect. The bottle is from the 1940s.

SPICY APPLE BLOSSOM perfume by Lander Co., Inc. NY, NY. The bottle from the 1940s is 3.75ml (1/8oz.).

TRULY YOURS perfume by Lander Co., Inc. NY, NY. "LANDER" is molded into the bottom of the 15ml (1/2oz.) bottle, which dates from the 1960s.

SWEET PEA perfume by Langlois. NY, NY. Langlois, a subsidiary of United Drug of Boston, MA. The bottle is from the 1960s. 3ml (.1oz.).

ARPEGE eau de parfum by Parfums Lanvin. Lanvin Couture House was established by Jeanne Lanvin in Paris, France. Lanvin introduced perfumes in 1923. The beautiful round bottle with a gold cap and a gold Lanvin logo is a 1993 edition. The bottle is based on an original black and gold design by Armand Rateau. The 5ml (.17oz.) bottle contains a floral-aldehyde fragrance, introduced in 1927.

ARPEGE and MY SIN extrait de Lanvin by Parfums Lanvin. Paris, France. The 7.5ml (1/4oz.) bottles are from the 1950s. They have gold foil labels and black stoppers. "LANVIN, FRANCE, NET CONTENTS 1/4 FL. OZ., LANVIN PARFUMS, NY IMPORTERS" is molded into the bottom of each bottle. MY SIN, a floral-aldehyde fragrance, was created in 1923.

VIA LANVIN parfum by Parfums Lanvin. Paris, France. The 3.75ml (1/8oz.) bottle has a green screw on stopper cap. The fragrance was introduced in 1946.

FANTASME eau de toilette by Parfums Ted Lapidus. Paris, France. A floral-fruity fragrance. 4.5ml (.15oz.).

Below: ALIAGE sport fragrance by Estee Lauder. NY, NY. The chypre-green fragrance introduced in 1972 is contained by a 3.75ml (1/8oz.) vial from the 1970s.

ALIAGE fragrance by Estee Lauder. NY, NY. 4.4ml (.15oz.).

AZURRE fragrance by Estee Lauder. NY, NY. A chypre-floral animalic fragrance introduced in 1969. Two different shaped bottles. 3.7ml (.12oz.).

CINNABAR perfume by Estee Lauder. NY, NY. A gold paper label on a 6.7ml (.22oz.) Wheaton glass bottle. An oriental-spicy fragrance introduced in 1978.

CINNABAR
perfume by
Estee Lauder.
NY, NY.
3.7ml (.12oz.).

ESTEE super perfume
by Estee Lauder. NY,
NY. 3.7ml (.12oz.). The
floral fragrance was
introduced in 1968.

YOUTH-DEW perfume by Estee Lauder.
NY, NY. A 3.7ml (.12oz.) frosted bottle with
an opaque flower stopper. The oriental-
ambery fragrance was introduced in 1953.

LAUREN cologne by Parfums Ralph Lauren.
Paris, France. Distributed by Warner-Lauren
Co. NY, NY. The 7.5ml (1/4oz.) ruby glass
bottle contains a floral-fruity fragrance
introduced in 1978.

Y perfume by Yves Saint Laurent Parfums. Paris, France. The two 1.87ml (1/16oz.) bottles have different letter colors. The brown-lettered bottle has "FRANCE" molded into the bottom. A chypre-fruity fragrance, Y was introduced in 1964.

CHAMPAGNE eau de toilette by Yves Saint Laurent Parfums. Paris, France. The 7.5ml (.26oz.) spray flacon contains a floral-fruity fragrance introduced in 1993. Is it perfume, or wine? The French courts will decide.

OPIUM parfum and eau de toilette by Yves Saint Laurent. Paris, France. 3.5ml (.12oz.) parfum. The Opium label is missing from the 7.5ml (1/4oz.) edt bottle. The "HP" trademark is on the bottom of each bottle. OPIUM an oriental-spicy fragrance, was introduced in 1977.

PARIS eau de toilette by Yves Saint Laurent. Paris, France. 7.5ml (1/4oz.). The faceted bottle comes with a hard-to-find pink cap. A floral fragrance, introduced in 1984.

LAZELL'S JOCKEY CLUB by Lazell. NY, NY. and Newburg, NY. A bottle from the turn of the century. A jester tag is attached to the bottle. "LAZELL'S PERFUMES, NEW YORK" is molded into the reverse side of the bottle and "BOTTLE PAT'D AUG 2ND 1887" is molded into the bottom.

DESERT FLOWER pefume by Leigh American Perfumers. NY, NY. A division of Shulton. The 1.87ml (1/16oz.) bottle has an etched flower on the front. The fragrance was introduced in 1947.

INDISCRET perfume by Lucien Lelong. Paris, France and Chicago, IL. Lucien Lelong introduced perfumes in 1924. INDISCRET was introduced in 1935. The ribbed 7.5ml (1/4oz.) bottle has a gold paper label and "LUCIEN LELONG, MADE IN FRANCE" molded into the bottom.

SIROCCO perfume by Lucien Lelong. Paris, France; Chicago, IL; NY, NY. The fragrance was introduced in 1934. The purse flacon holds 4ml (1.25 drams, or .13oz.).

TAILSPIN perfume by Lucien Lelong. Paris, France and NY, NY. The 5ml (.15oz.) bottle has a label on the bottom. The fragrance was introduced in 1940.

CONFETTI perfume by Lentheric Perfumes. Paris, France; Chicago, IL; NY, NY. 1.87ml (1/16oz.). CONFETTI was introduced in 1939.

CONFETTI perfume by Lentheric Perfumes. Paris, France; Chicago, IL; NY, NY. 3.75ml (1/8oz.).

SHANGHAI perfume by Lentheric Perfumes. Paris, France; Chicago, IL; NY, NY. The 15ml (1/2oz.) glass bottle has a plastic stopper. The fragrance was introduced in 1936.

TWEED perfume by Lentheric Perfumes. Paris, France; Chicago, IL; NY, NY. Lentheric, founded by Guillaume Lentheric, dates back to 1795. TWEED was introduced in 1935 and was their most popular fragrance. The 1.87ml (1/16oz.) bottle has "TWEED" molded into the glass, and the 3.75ml (1/8oz.) bottle has a gold paper label.

FASHION parfum de Leonard Parfums. Paris, France. The 1.87ml (1/16oz.) bottle has "LEONARD, FRANCE" molded into the bottom.

Left: LEONARD DE LEONARD eau de toilette by Leonard Parfums. Paris, France. The floral-green fragrance was introduced in 1989 and is contained in a 4ml (1/8oz.) bottle.

Right: DIAMONDS AND RUBIES by Liz Taylor and Parfums International, Ltd. NY, NY. This 5ml (.17oz.) bottle came in an inexpensive set. The floral-oriental fragrance was introduced in 1993.

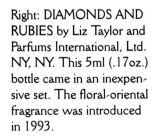

PASSION parfum by Liz Taylor and Parfums International, Ltd. NY, NY. The floral-semi oriental fragrance was introduced in 1987. This 3.7ml (.12oz.) bottle is now clear glass with a colored fragrance and the diamond is not painted gold.

LILAS 19 perfume by Parfum L'Orle, Inc. NY, NY. This perfumery was very active in the 1940s. 4ml (.13oz.)

LOVABLE parfum by Lovable Cosmetics Inc. NY, NY. 3.75ml (1/8oz.) The bottle has a gold paper label.

NUIT DE LONGCHAMP parfum by Lubin. Pierre-Francios Lubin established the perfumery in 1798 in Paris, France. "FRANCE" is molded into the bottom of the 1.87ml (1/16oz.) bottle. The fragrance was introduced in 1935.

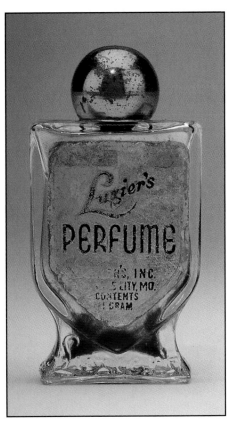

LUCIANO SOPRANI eau de toilette by Luciano Soprani Profumi.
Milan, Italy. The 5ml (.17oz.) bottle is a Dinand design.

LUZIER'S perfume by Luzier's Inc. Kansas City, MO.
The 3.75ml (1/8oz.) bottle is from the 1940s.
"LUZIER'S" is molded into the bottom of the bottle.

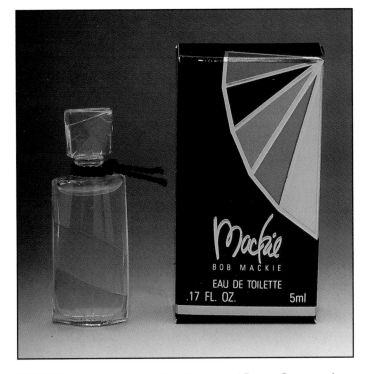

FANTASIA by Lynette. NY, NY. The
fragrance was introduced in 1943. 3.75ml
(1/8oz.).

MACKIE eau de toilette by Bob Mackie and Rivera Concepts Inc.
Beverly Hills, CA. Hollywood designer Bob Mackie introduced
this floral-oriental fragrance in 1991. The bottle, designed by
Pierre Dinand and Bob Mackie, holds 5ml (.17oz.).

ONLY CRAZY eau de toilette for women by Julio Iglesias and Mas Cosmetics. Barcelona, Spain. 10ml (.3oz.) The bottle has "ONLY" on the front; "CRAZY" appears neither on the label or bottle.

MADELEINE DE MADELEINE parfum by Madeleine Mono Ltd. London, England. The floral fragrance was introduced in 1978 and is contained in a 5ml (.17oz.) bottle.

YESTERDAY eau de toilette by Marbert. Dusseldorf, Germany. 7.5ml (1/4oz.). The bottle has gold letters.

VOLAGE parfum by Neiman Marcus. Dallas, TX. The frosted glass bottle with a frosted stopper holds 3.75ml (1/8oz.).

PRINCESS MARINA DE BOURBON eau de toilette by Parfums Princess Marina De Bourbon Parme. Paris, France. The 7.5ml (1/4oz.) bottle has "HP" on the bottom.

SILENT NIGHT perfume by Countess Maritza. NY, NY. The fragrance was introduced in 1947. This 7.5ml (1/4oz.) bottle is from the same era.

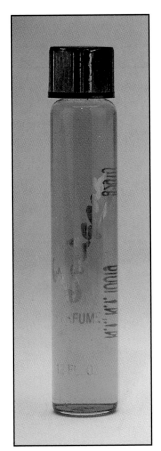

ENIGMA perfume by Alexander de Markoff Ltd. (Martin De Botelito). NY, NY. The chypre fragrance was introduced in 1972. 3.7ml (.12oz.).

NO REGRETS perfume by Alexander de Markoff Ltd. NY, NY. The firm has been active since 1939. The 1.7ml (.06oz.) bottle has "SGD" molded into the bottom. The bottle comes in a gold paper pouch featuring many quotations about love.

EPRIS perfume by Max Factor. Hollywood, CA. 3.7ml (.12oz.).

GOLDEN WOODS bath perfume by Max Factor. Hollywood, CA; London, England; Paris, France. 1.87ml (1/16oz.). The fragrance was introduced in 1951.

TOUJOURS MOI eau de parfum by Max Factor. Hollywood CA. 15ml (1/2oz.).

PHEROMONE perfume by Marilyn Miglin. Chicago, IL. The 3.75ml (1/8oz.) bottle comes in a gold bag. Marilyn Miglin proclaims this to be "The world's precious perfume. Created for the woman who makes life an adventure. With love, M.M." The green fragrance was introduced in 1980.

PHEROMONE SACRED OIL by Marilyn Miglin. Chicago, IL. The 6ml (1/5oz.) bottle has Marilyn Miglin's signature in gold.

MOLTO MISSONI eau de toilette by Missoni. Distributed by Orlane. Paris, France and NY, NY. The 3.5ml (.12oz.) hexagonal bottle contains an oriental-ambery fragrance.

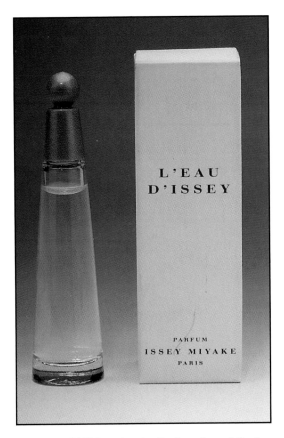

L'EAU D'ISSEY parfum by Parfums Issey Miyake and Beaute Prestige International. Paris, France. The 3ml (.1oz.) bottle contains a floral-fruity fragrance.

CONCRETA MUGUET by Parfums Molinard. Established in Paris by Molinard in 1849. The fragrance was introduced in 1925. 1.87ml (1/16oz.).

RAFALE parfum by Parfums Molinard. Paris, France. 1.87ml (1/16oz.).

VIVRE parfum by Molyneux. Paris, France. The couture house was established in 1919 by Edward Molyneux. Perfumes were introduced in 1925. VIVRE was introduced in 1971. 1.87ml (1/16oz.)

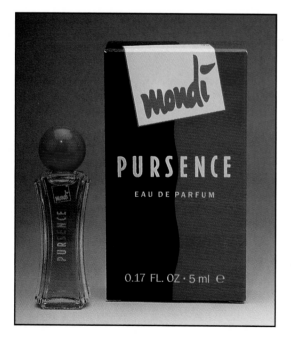

MONTANA D'ELLE eau de parfum by Claude Montana Parfums. Distributed by Prestige Fragrances, Ltd. NY, NY. 2.5ml (.08oz.).

PURSENCE eau de parfum by Mondi and DC Design Cosmetics. Munich, Germany. 5ml (.17oz.)

BAKIR cologne by Germaine Monteil Cosmetics Corporation. NY, NY. 15ml (1/2oz.).

CHAMPAGNE eau de toilette by Germaine Monteil Cosmetics Corporation. NY, NY. 6ml (.19oz.).

FLEUR SAUVAGE parfum by Germaine Monteil Cosmetics Corporation. NY, NY. "M" is on the bottom of the 3ml (.1oz.) bottle. The fragrance was introduced in 1953.

GALORE bath perfume pour le bain by Germaine Monteil Cosmetics Corporation. NY, NY. The 15ml (1/2oz.) frosted glass bottle contains a floral-oriental fragrance introduced in 1964.

MAGNETIC by Gabriela Sabatini and Muelhens Inc. Distributed from Orange, CT. 3ml (.1oz.). Sabatini, a famous tennis player, introduced the floral-fruity fragrance in 1993.

ANGEL eau de parfum by Thierry Mugler Parfums, Etoile Collection. Neuilly, France. The oriental fragrance was introduced in 1993. The star-shaped 4ml (.14oz.) flacon is by Brosse.

DECOLLETE eau de toilette by Merle Norman Cosmetics. Los Angeles, CA. 4ml (.14oz.)

VIVONS parfum by Merle Norman Cosmetics. Los Angeles, CA. 1.87ml (1/16oz.).

UNE CARESSE by Oberon. Paris, France. A beautiful clear glass bottle with flowers engraved in the front and back. An ornate cap made of silver metal holds a glass dauber. The bottle has "HP, MADE IN FRANCE" molded into the bottom, and slips into a pink felt sleeve. 3.75ml (1/8oz.).

TRISTANO ONOFRI eau de parfum by Tristano Onofri. Dusseldorf, Germany. The 4ml (.13oz.) glass bottle has an opaque ribboned stopper.

SOLO TU eau de parfum by Tristano Onofri. Dusseldorf, Germany; Paris, France; Geneva, Switzerland. The 5ml (.17oz.) colbalt blue bottle has gold lettering and a blue ribboned stopper.

PERFUME #1 by Orgel Brothers. Distributed from Washington, DC. 3.75ml (1/8oz.).

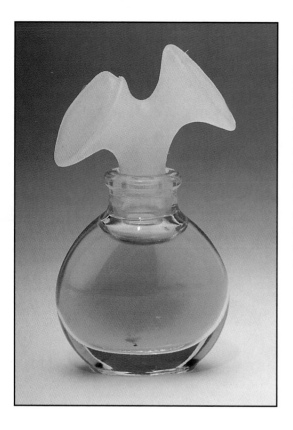

CHLOE parfum by Parfums International Ltd. NY, NY. CHLOE was created by Karl Lagerfeld and introduced in 1975. The floral fragrance is contained in a 3.7ml (.12oz.) bottle with opaque lilies as a stopper. "CHLOE" is molded into the bottom of the bottle.

K L parfum by Karl Lagerfeld, distributed by Parfums International Ltd. NY, NY. An oriental-spicy fragrance introduced in 1983. 5ml (.17oz.).

Left: SUN MOON STARS LAGERFELD parfum by Parfums International Ltd. NY, NY. The 3.7ml (.12oz.) round midnight blue bottle has a sun, a cresent moon, and stars. The fragrance was introduced in 1994.

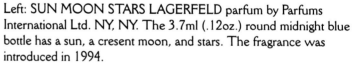

Right: WHITE SHOULDERS parfum by Parfums International Ltd. NY, NY. The 3.75ml (1/8oz.) bottle is from an inexpensive set.

WHITE SHOULDERS parfum by Parfums International Ltd. NY, NY. 7.5ml (1/4oz.). The floral fragrance was introduced in 1935 by Evyan.

ADVENTURE perfume by Park & Tilford. NY, NY. 7.75ml (.27oz.). The fragrance was introduced in 1937.

CHERISH perfume by Park & Tilford. NY, NY. 3.75ml (1/8oz.). Introduced in 1938.

DESIRE perfume by Park & Tilford. NY, NY. 3ml (.85 dram) and 9ml (.31oz.) Introduced in 1938.

Left: HONEY-SUCKLE deluxe cologne by Park & Tilford. NY, NY. 15ml (1/2oz.) The bottle is from the 1940s.

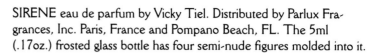

SIRENE eau de parfum by Vicky Tiel. Distributed by Parlux Fragrances, Inc. Paris, France and Pompano Beach, FL. The 5ml (.17oz.) frosted glass bottle has four semi-nude figures molded into it.

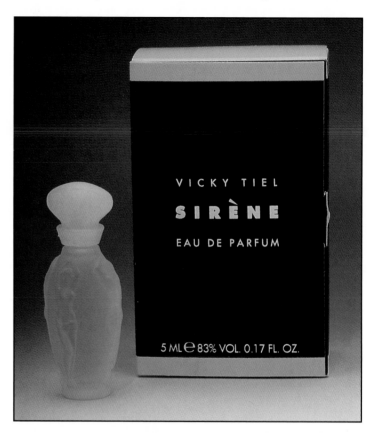

TODD OLDHAM fragrance for women, eau de parfum by Todd Oldham and Parlux Fragrances, Inc. NY, NY and Pompano Beach, FL. A floral-fruity fragrance contained in a 6.5ml (.2oz.) bottle.

1000 eau de parfum by Jean Patou Parfumer. Paris, France. 7ml (.23oz.). The floral fragrance introduced in 1972 was called "the essence of extravagance" by Jean Patou. "JEAN PATOU, MADE IN FRANCE" is molded into the bottom of the green marbled bottle. The red cap is attached to a green glass dauber. This bottle design is also used for JOY by Jean Patou.

COCKTAIL DRY parfum by Jean Patou Parfumer. Paris, France. The fragrance was introduced in 1930. "JP" is on the cap. 3ml (.1oz.).

JOY parfum by Jean Patou Parfumer. Paris, France. 7ml (.23oz.). The classic black glass Jean Patou bottle has a red cap attached to a black glass dauber. Introduced in 1930 as "the most expensive perfume in the world." A floral fragrance.

When purchasing a new fragrance, take a coffee bean with you to sniff before smelling each new fragrance.

SUBLIME eau de parfum by Jean Patou Parfumer. Paris, France. A gold-tinted fragrance in a sunburst gold box. 4ml (.14oz.). A floral fragrance introduced in 1993.

ROSES OF PLATINUM cologne by Dorothy Perkins Co., Inc. St. Louis, MO. 3.75ml (1/8oz.). The company was active in the 1930s.

SAMBA NOVA eau de toilette by The Perfumer's Workshop, Ltd. Paris, France. 7.5ml (1/2oz.). The clear bottle has "SAMBA" on the bottom. A floral-oriental fragrance.

ENGLISH SPICE perfumed cologne by Arthur Philippi. NY, NY. 15ml (1/2oz.). "APH" is molded into the bottom of the bottle.

GARDENIA perfume by Arthur Philippi. NY, NY. 7.5ml (1/4oz.) A circled "S" is on the bottom of the bottle.

BANDIT parfum by Parfums Robert Piguet. Paris, France. Robert Piguet Couture House was established in 1933 and introduced perfumes in 1939. This chypre-floral animalic fragrance was introduced in 1944. The glass bottle and stopper is from the late 1940s or 1950-1951. It has "HP, ROBERT PIGUET, BOTTLE MADE IN FRANCE" molded into the bottom, and measures 7.5ml (1/4oz.). The firm closed in 1951.

CALYPSO parfum by Parfums Robert Piguet. Paris, France. "ROBERT PIGUET FRANCE, HP" is marked on the bottom of the 1.87ml (1/16oz.) bottle. CALYPSO was introduced in 1959.

FRACAS parfum by Parfums Robert Piguet. Paris, France. The floral fragrance, developed in Occupied France during World War II, was introduced in 1945. 4ml (.13oz.).

FLIRTATION perfume by Ed Pinaud. Paris, France. 3.75ml (1/8oz.). A gold paper label is used on the bottle. The fragrance was introduced in 1944. The perfumery dates from the early 1800s.

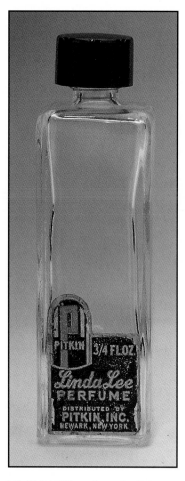

LINDA LEE perfume by Pitkin, Inc. Newark, NJ and NY, NY. 22.5ml (3/4oz.).

POOLE'S PERFUME PRETENDERS II by Poole's Beauty Boutique. NY, NY. 5ml (.15oz.).

HOT perfume by Bill Blass and Prestige Fragrances, Ltd. NY, NY. An oriental fragrance in a red box. 3.75ml (1/8oz.).

BELOVED and PROPHECY perfume by Prince Matchabelli, Inc. NY, NY. Shown with the Prince Matchabelli Crown bottle in gold over black. The company was established in 1926 by Prince George Matchabelli, and the crown-shaped bottles were introduced in 1928. BELOVED was introduced in 1950 in a 1.87ml (1/16oz.) bottle, PROPHECY in 1974 in a 3.75ml (1/8oz.) bottle.

ABANO perfumed bath oil by Prince Matchabelli, Inc. NY, NY. The scepter bottle holds 7.5ml (1/4oz.) The crown bottle holds 1.87ml (1/16oz.). ABANO bath oil was introduced in 1938.

AVIANCE perfume by Prince Matchabelli, Inc. NY, NY. Distributed from Greenwich, CT. 3.75ml (1/8oz.). The fragrance was introduced in 1962.

AVIANCE NIGHT MUSK by Prince Matchabelli, Inc. NY, NY and Greenwich, CT. 7.5ml (1/4oz.).

CACHET perfume by Prince Matchabelli, Inc. Greenwich, CT. 3.75ml (1/8oz.). The fragrance was introduced in 1970.

CACHET cologne
by Prince
Matchabelli, Inc.
Greenwich, CT.
7.5ml (1/4oz.).

WIND SONG
cologne by Prince
Matchabelli, Inc. NY,
NY. A scepter bottle.
7.5ml (1/4oz.). The
fragrance was
introduced in 1953.

WIND SONG perfume by Prince
Matchabelli, Inc. Greenwich, CT. 7.5ml
(1/4oz.).

IL BACIO parfum by Princess Marcella Borghese. NY, NY. The floral-fruity
fragrance, introduced in 1993, is contained in a bottle designed by Marc
Rosen. "IL BACIO" and "The kiss, where it all began," is inscribed on the
box. 3.6ml (1/8oz.).

WALLIS eau de toilette by Parfums Princesse Wallis. Paris, France. The 10ml (1/3oz.) bottle is inscribed "WALLIS." The box shows a beautiful ruby ring, and the bottle is in the shape of a gold ring and a large ruby stopper. The fragrance was named for Wallis Simpson, who was married to the Duke of Windsor.

G GIGLI eau de toilette by Romeo Gigli and Proteo Profumi. Milan, Italy. The G GIGLI fragrance bottle comes in a red paper roll box. 7.5ml (1/4oz.).

FIORILU eau de parfum by Pupa Parfums. Milan, Italy. 4ml (.13oz.) The frosted bottle has a frosted rose stopper.

FIORILU eau de parfum by Pupa Parfums. Milan, Italy. The 4ml (.13oz.) bottle contains a pink fragrance and sits in a frosted plastic leaf. Boxed in a pink plastic base and a clear plastic cover.

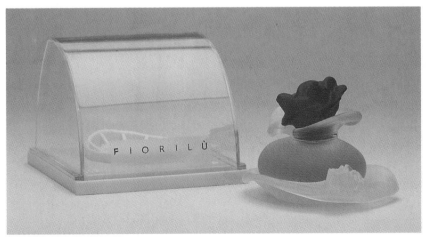

REPLIQUE parfum by Raphael. Paris, France. The couture introduced perfumes after 1936. The red pouch holds a 3.75ml (1/8oz.) glass bottle. A gold braided string holds the glass stopper. "R" is on the red seal. The bottle has "RAPHAEL, MADE IN FRANCE, HP" molded into the bottom. REPLIQUE was introduced in 1944.

PIQUE cologne by Redken Labs Inc. Canoga Park, CA. The 3.75ml (1/8oz.) bottle has an opaque plastic stopper in the shape of a butterfly

REPLIQUE parfum by Raphael. Paris, France. "FRANCE, HP" is molded into the 1.87ml (1/16oz.) bottle.

ALINE perfume by Maison Renee. Hollywood, CA. The black glass bottle holds 6ml (.2oz.).

SWEET PEA perfume by Renaud. Paris, France. Distributed in the U.S.A. from Boston, MA. Renaud was established in Paris in 1817. The small vial-type bottle is inscribed "MADE IN GERMANY," with black stripes on it. The brass cap is double stamped "GERMANY." The metal-hinged box is lined inside with velvet and satin, while the outside is covered with a green material. 3ml (.1oz.).

TURBULENCES parfum de toilette by Parfums Revillon. Paris, France. The 2ml (1/14oz.) bottle contains a floral fragrance introduced in 1981.

DETCHEMA perfume by Parfums Revillon. Paris, France. The perfumery was established in 1932, and this fragrance was introduced in 1953. 1.5ml (1/16oz.).

JONTUE perfume by Revlon. NY, NY. "HP" is molded into the bottom of the 3.75ml (1/8oz.) bottle. The fragrance was introduced in 1975.

WILD HEART cologne by Revlon Consumer Product Corporation. NY, NY. 4.44ml (.15oz.) An ad states "It's not love if it's not wild."

IRICE bottle by I.W. Rice. NY, NY. The cut glass bottle has a jeweled brass cap with a glass dauber. The tag is stamped "Czechoslovakia." 7.5ml (1/4oz.).

CAPRICCI parfum by Parfums Nina Ricci. Paris, France. "MADE IN FRANCE" is molded into the bottom of the mini Marc Lalique bottle from 1961. With brass cap and tag, the bottle holds 1.87ml (1/16oz.). The floral fragrance was introduced in 1961.

CAPRICCI eau de toilette by Parfums Nina Ricci. Paris, France. "LALIQUE, FRANCE" is molded into the bottom of the round bottle with a plastic cap. 7.5ml (1/4oz.).

COEUR JOIE parfum by Parfums Nina Ricci. Paris, France. This was the first fragrance introduced by Nina Ricci, a floral fragrance, it was introduced in 1946. The 7.5ml (1/4oz.) bottle has "LALIQUE, FRANCE" molded into the bottom.

FAROUCHE parfum by Parfums Nina Ricci. Paris, France. The frosted wings bottle was designed by Marc Lalique for FAROUCHE in 1974. "HP" is molded into the bottom of the 3ml (.1oz.) bottle. The floral-aldehyde fragrance was introduced in 1974.

FAROUCHE eau de toilette by Parfums Nina Ricci. Paris, France and NY, NY. The bottle, designed by Marc Lalique, was originally used for L'AIR DU TEMPS in the 1950s. "BOTTLE MADE IN FRANCE" is molded into the bottom of the bottle. 10ml (1/3oz.).

FLEUR DE FLEURS parfum by Parfums Nina Ricci. Paris, France. A frosted flower stopper in a Lalique flacon. "HP" is molded into the bottom of the 3.75ml (1/8oz.) bottle. The floral-aldehyde fragrance was introduced in 1980.

L'AIR DU TEMPS perfume and eau de toilette by Parfums Nina Ricci. Paris, France. A miniature copy of the original sunburst bottle designed by Lalique for L'AIR DU TEMPS in 1948. The bottle with a brass cap has a tag that states, "Distributed in the U.S.A. by J. Cochran Inc. NY, NY." The other 1.87ml (1/16oz.) bottle has a gold-colored cap.

NINA eau de toilette by Parfums Nina Ricci. Paris, France. A copy of the original design with a gold-colored cap. "NINA RICCI 6ml" is molded into the bottom of the 6ml (.20oz.) bottle.

NINA parfum by Parfums Nina Ricci. Paris, France. The beautiful draped glass flacon is an original 1987 design by Marie Claude Lalique. The floral fragrance was introduced in 1987. 7.5ml (1/4oz.).

FRANCETTE by Paul Rieger Perfumer. San Francisco, CA. The glass stopper is sealed in a classic bottle, from the 1920s. "GERMANY" is molded into the bottom, and a gold foil label adorns the the front, and "$1.00 size" is printed on the back of the box. 6ml (.2oz.).

GODDESS OF CRETE by Rilling Dermetics Co. NY, NY. Introduced in 1947, the twenty perfume nips are contained in a gold paper-covered tube and tube cover. Included are instructions on how to use the nips.

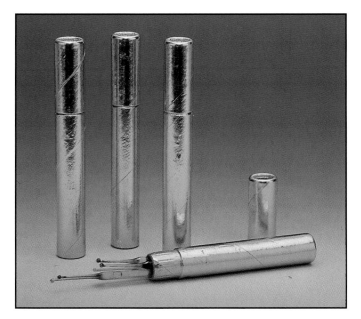

Perfume nips were perfume samples popular in the 1940s and 1950s. The four gold paper tubes hold different fragrances, identified by the color on the bottom of the container. Included is a piece of paper with printed instructions on how to use the nips: Snap off both slender ends of the plastene tubes, then apply.

EAU DE ROCHAS eau de toilette by Parfums Rochas. Marcel Rochas Couture House was established in 1925 in Paris, France. The chypre-fresh fragrance was introduced in 1970. 10ml (.34oz.).

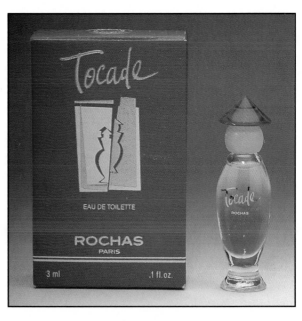

MYSTERE eau de parfum by Parfums Rochas. Paris, France. Distributed from NY, NY. An oblique shaped bottle design by R. Grani and S. Mansau. 3.75ml (1/8oz.). The perfume, introduced in 1978, is a chypre-floral animalic fragrance.

TOCADE eau de toilette by Parfums Rochas. Paris, France. The fragrance, introduced in 1994, is contained in a 3ml (.1oz.) bottle.

8e JOUR ("8th Day") eau de toilette by Yves Rocher. La Gacilly, France. The frosted amber bottle with a blue cap holds 7.5ml (1/4oz.).

NUIT D'ORCHIDEE eau de toilette by Yves Rocher. La Gacilly, France. 7.5ml (1/4oz.) A cobalt blue bottle with a blue, gold-flecked cap and gold lettering.

ORCHIDEE eau de toilette by Yves Rocher. La Gacilly, France. 7.5ml (1/4oz.). A gold-colored fragrance in a gold-flecked bottle and cap.

PIVONE eau de toilette by Yves Rocher. La Gacilly, France. 7.5ml (1/4oz.). The fragrance is contained in a milk glass bottle with an opaque pink flower stopper.

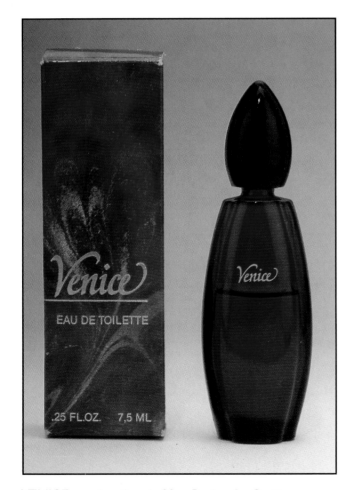

VENICE eau de toilette by Yves Rocher. La Gacilly, France. The ruby glass bottle has a black cap and holds 7.5ml (1/4oz.).

VIE PRIVEE eau de toilette by Yves Rocher. La Gacilly, France. The green frosted bottle has a frosted stopper and holds 7.5ml (1/4oz.).

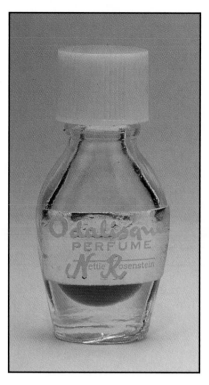

ODALISQUE perfume by Nettie Rosenstein. NY, NY. The fragrance contained in this 1.5ml (1/16oz.) bottle was introduced in 1946.

LILY OF THE VALLEY perfume by Ronni. Distributed by Parfums Ronni. NY, NY. The two bottles have slightly different labels. From the 1920s. 7.5ml (1/4oz.).

GARDENIA perfume by Royal Perfumers, Inc. NY, NY. The gold paper label on the cut glass bottle has a gold painted metal cap designed as a crown. 3.75ml (1/8oz.).

BARYNIA eau de parfum by Parfums Helena Rubinstein. Paris, France. The glass bottle has a cube as a stopper. 5ml (.17oz.).

COURANT eau de parfum by Parfums Helena Rubinstein. Paris, France. The 15ml (1/2oz.) bottle is inscribed "BOTTLE MADE IN ITALY" on the bottom.

EMOTION cologne by Parfums Helena Rubinstein. Made in England for American Fromatics Inc. Secaucus, NJ. The fragrance was introduced in 1966. 7.5ml (1/4oz.).

HEAVEN SENT eau de parfum by Parfums Helena Rubinstein. Paris, France. The 15ml (1/2oz.) glass bottle has a swirled pattern and a blue cap, from the early 1960s. The fragrance was introduced in 1941.

RUSSIAN perfume oil. The glass vial inside has a gold label and a plastic cap. The wooden case is inscribed "PO3A" and "ECEHUNDR" in Russian.

JIL SANDER
perfume by Jil
Sander Cosmetics. Wiesbaden,
Germany. 7.5ml
(1/4oz.).

SAYIDATY eau de parfum by Sayidaty. England. 7ml (.23oz.).

IMPERIAL DANISH MUSK perfume by Scandia International Ltd.
NY, NY. 3.75ml (1/8oz.).

SCHERRER eau de parfum by Parfums Jean-Louis
Scherrer. Paris, France. Distributed by Parfums
International Ltd. NY, NY. "HP" is molded into the
bottom of the 3.7ml (1/8oz.) bottle. A chypre
fragrance.

DANCE ARROGANCE eau de toilette by Parfums Schiaparelli. Distributed by Benessere Pikenz. Milan, Italy. 5ml (.16oz.).

SHOCKING parfum by Parfums Schiaparelli. Paris, France. Schiaparelli Couture House was established in 1928 by Elsa Schiaparelli. "FRANCE" is molded into the bottom of the 1.87ml (1/16oz.) bottle. This oriental fragrance was introduced in 1936.

SHOCKING YOU parfum by Parfums Schiaparelli. Paris, France. 20ml (3/4oz.). A modern floral fragrance introduced in 1977.

> It is best not to try more than three scents at one time.

EXTRA perfume by Schissler. 3.75ml (1/8oz.). The bottle has a cork stopper and dates from the early 1920s.

DESIGN parfum by Paul Sebastian, Inc. Distributed from Ocean, NJ. The 7.5ml (1/4oz.) bottle has "HP" molded into the bottom and is a floral-fruity fragrance, introduced in 1986.

APPLE BLOSSOM extrait by C.H. Selick Perfumer. NY, NY. 15ml (1/2oz.). "S" is molded into the back of the bottle. The stopper is a sprinkler-type and has "SELICK'S" in raised letters on the metal part. A series of 1914-1/4 United States Internal Revenue stamps is on the side of the bottle.

INOUI perfume mist by Shiseido Cosmetics. Tokyo, Japan. Founded by Shiseido Ginza as a pharmaceutical company in 1872. Distributed by America Ltd. NY, NY. The case holds a 7.5ml (1/4oz.) replaceable metal spray cartridge. The fragrance was introduced in 1959.

TAJI perfume oil by Shulton. NY, NY and Clifton, NJ. Shulton was established in 1934 by William Schultz. The fragrance was introduced in 1965. 3.75ml (1/8oz.).

PARFIQUE perfume by Parfum Similaire, Inc. Kenilworth, NJ. 7.5ml (1/4oz.).

ROSE perfume by Spencer Perfume Co. South Bend, IN. The glass bottle holds 15ml (1/2oz.) and has a glass and cork stopper. The bottle is from the 1920s.

LADY CATHERINE perfume by Stanley Home Products. Westfield, MA. The fragrance was introduced in 1952. The purse flacon was used for different scents produced by the company. The products were sold to homemakers by door to door salesmen. 3.75ml (1/8oz.)

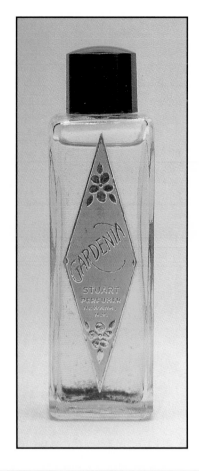

GARDENIA perfume by Stewart Perfumer. Newark, NJ. and NY, NY. The 15ml (1/2oz.) bottle has a gold paper label and is from the 1950s.

RUSSIAN; RUSSE; RUSSICH eau de cologne by Bruno Storp. Munich, Germany. The 15ml (1/2oz.) bottle is from the 1930s.

A set of four half-dram bottles that were sold in a set by Stuart Products Co. This set was usually inexpensive, sold in dime stores in the 1940s.

MILADY'S STRIKE perfume by Stuart Products Co. The company was founded in 1935 by William B. Cohen in St. Paul, MN. The 3.75ml (1/8oz.) bottle is glass with a wooden screw-on cap that forms a bowling pin.

Below: GARDENIA perfume by Teel. 15ml (1/2oz.).
A dime store fragrance from the 1940s.

GARDENIA perfume by
Tre-Jur. The firm was
established in New York
by Albert Mosheim in
1934. NY, NY and Paris,
France. 7.5ml (1/4oz.).
The gold paper label
reads "1 cent WITH
PURCHASE OF 3
CAMAY." The fragrance
was introduced in 1936.

MY TREASURE perfume by Treasure Masters Perfume. The
3.7ml (.12oz.) bottle comes in a box that includes a sachet
pillow.

TRUSSARDI eau de toilette by Trussardi Parfums. Milan, Italy.
7.5ml (1/4oz.). The white hobnail bottle has a Trussardi label.

MIDNIGHT and OPTIMISTE perfumes by Tussy, Len & Fink Products Corporation. Bloomfield, NJ. MIDNIGHT was introduced in 1950 and OPTIMISTE in 1949. Here, they are connected by the double cap. The scent names are in gold lettering. Tussy was founded in Paris by Joseph Lesquendieu in 1882, and purchased in 1928 by Lehn & Fink.

JUNGLE GARDENIA perfume by Tuvache, Inc. NY, NY. The 1.87ml (1/16oz.) bottle has a gold paper label. A circled "L" is molded into the bottom of the bottle. The fragrance was introduced in 1932.

JUNGLE GARDENIA perfume by Tuvache, Inc. NY, NY. Imported from England and distributed from Fort Lauderdale FL. 10ml (.3oz.).

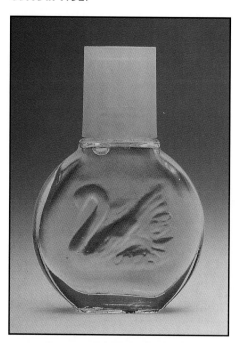

VANDERBILT perfume by Gloria Vanderbilt. Distributed by Cosmair, Inc. NY, NY. VANDERBILT was created in 1982 to honor the family name. The floral-oriental fragrance is contained in a 3ml (.1oz.) bottle. The bottle design is by Bernard Kotyuk.

ALURIA perfume and natural powder by Lucretia Vanderbilt. NY,
NY. A 3.75ml (1/8oz.) bottle. The set is from the 1930s.

LUCRETIA
VANDERBILT
perfume by Lucretia
Vanderbilt. NY, NY.
3.75ml (1/8oz.). The
bottle is from the
1930s.

UGO VANELLI eau de parfum by Parfums Ugo Vanelli. Paris,
France. 3.5ml (.1oz.). The bottle contains a floral-fruity fragrance.
"UV" is on the bottom of the bottle.

FOLLOW ME perfume by Varva. NY,
NY. FOLLOW ME ("Suivez Moi"). The
3.75ml (1/8oz.) bottle is from the 1940s.
The fragrance was introduced in 1943.

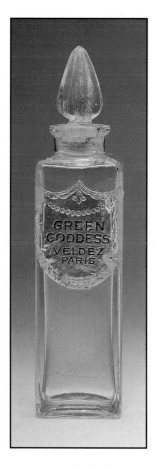

GREEN GODDESS perfume by Veldez. Paris, France. The 7.5ml (1/4oz.) glass bottle has a silver paper label.

VERSUS eau de toilette by Gianni Versace, Versace Profumi. Milan, Italy. Distributed by Vapro U.S.A. Ltd. NY, NY. The 3.5ml (.11oz.) ruby glass bottle has "SDG" molded into the bottom. The floral-fruity fragrance was introduced in 1992.

RAPTURE perfume by Victoria's Secret. The 3.75ml (1/8oz.) heart-shaped bottle has a red plastic stopper, and contains a floral-oriental fragrance.

A V eau de parfum by Adrienne Vittadini. Distributed by Heppa Beauty Group. NY, NY. 7.5ml (1/4oz.).

JE REVIENS parfum by Parfums Worth. Paris, France. "FRENCH BOTTLE" is molded into the bottom. 1.87ml (1/16oz.) The fragrance was introduced in 1932. Worth Couture House was established in 1858 by Charles Frederick Worth. Perfumes were introduced in 1924.

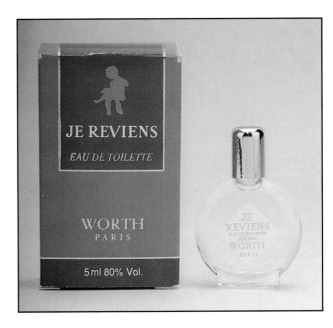

Above: JE REVIENS ("I will return") eau de toilette by Parfums Worth. Paris, France. 5ml (1/6oz.). A floral-aldehyde fragrance.

JE REVIENS eau de parfum by Parfums Worth. Paris, France. 7ml (.236oz.) The bottle is frosted glass with stars, and the frosted stopper is marked with a "W." The bottle is based on the original Rene Lalique design.

FRENCH LILAC cologne by Wrisley. The company was established in 1800 by Allen B. Wrisley. The Wheaton bottle holds 7.5ml (1/4oz.) and is from the 1950s.

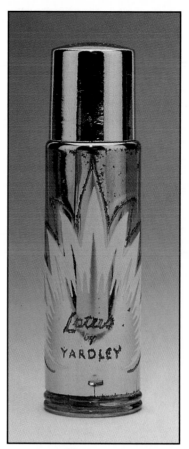

LOTUS perfume by Yardley & Co., Ltd. Yardley was founded as a pharmaceutical company in 1770 in London by Thomas Yardley. Distributed from NY, NY. The 3.75ml (1/8oz.) glass purse flacon is in a metal case.

LOTUS perfume by Yardley. London, England. 1.87ml (1/16oz.). The beautiful bottle contained a fragrance introduced in 1948.

ZIG ZAG parfum by Zsa Zsa. NY, NY. "BOTTLE MADE IN ITALY" is molded into the 7.5ml (1/4oz.) bottle.

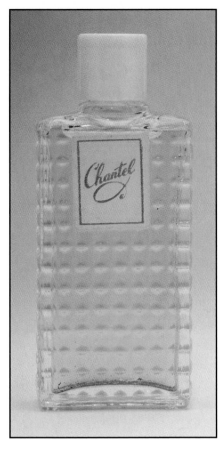

CHANTEL perfume. 15ml (1/2oz.).

LET'S DECIDE IT NOW perfume.
3.75ml (1/8oz.).

MELLOW-GLO perfume shown in two different 3.75ml (1/8oz.)
bottles.

SAMPAQUITA perfume. 3.75ml (1/8oz.).

ARAMIS eau de cologne for men by Aramis Inc. NY, NY. 15ml (1/2oz.). A chypre fragrance.

ARAMIS 900 cologne for men by Aramis Inc. NY, NY. 7.5ml (1/4oz.).

ARMANI eau pour homme by Giorgio Armani Parfums. A division of Cosmair, Inc. NY, NY. A Dinand design. 5ml (.17oz.). A citrus fragrance.

HO HANG eau de toilette pour homme by Balenciaga. Paris, France. The ribbed bottle is banded by the HO HANG label. 10ml (.3oz.).

BEETHOVEN eau de parfum pour homme by Parfums L.V. Beethoven. Paris, France. "SGB" is molded into the bottom of the 10ml (1/3oz.) bottle.

BIAGIOTTI UOMO eau de toilette pour homme by Laura Biagiotti. Eurocos. Italy. 5ml (.17oz.).

WITNESS eau de toilette pour homme by Parfums Jacques Bogart. Paris, France. The blue glass 4ml (.13oz.) bottle has "H" molded into the bottom.

BOIS DE VETIVER eau de toilette pour homme by Parfums Jacques Bogart. Paris, France. NY, NY. 3.5ml (1/8oz.).

EGOISTE PLATINUM eau de toilette pour homme by Chanel. Paris, France. 4ml (.13oz.). The woody fragrance was introduced in 1993.

POUR MONSIEUR eau de toilette concentree pour homme by Chanel. Paris, France. 4ml (.13oz.). The clear glass bottle has "CBG" molded into the bottom. A citrus fragrance.

CLAIBORNE cologne for men by Liz Claiborne Cosmetics, Inc. NY, NY. 15ml (1/2oz.).

CARLO CORINTO ROUGE eau de toilette pour homme by Parfums Carlo Corinto. Paris, France. 10ml (1/3oz.). The fragrance was introduced in 1991.

DEBONAIR aftershave lotion for men by Daggett & Ramsdell. Newark, NJ. Distributed by The Fuller Brush Co. Hartford, CT. 3.75ml (1/8oz.). The fragrance was introduced in 1949.

SALVADOR DALI eau de toilette pour homme by Parfums Salvador Dali. 5ml (.17oz.). A miniature of the original flacon. The bottle has the Salvador Dali signature on both front and back. The fragrance was introduced in 1981.

CANOE eau de cologne for men by Dana Parfums Corp. Paris, France. NY, NY. "NOT FOR SALE, MADE IN FRANCE" is molded into the back of the bottle. "DANA" is molded into the bottom of the 3.75ml (1/8oz.) bottle. CANOE was introduced in 1936.

RELAX eau de toilette pour homme by Parfums Davidoff. Paris, France. The green glass bottle holds 7.5ml (1/4oz.).

JULES aftershave lotion pour homme by Parfums Christian Dior. Paris, France. 9ml (1/3oz.). The fragrance was introduced in 1980.

DUNHILL eau de toilette for men by Alfred Dunhill Ltd. London, England. Parfums Cree in France. The 5ml (.16oz.) bottle has "DUNHILL" molded into the bottom.

BOSS eau de toilette pour homme by Hugo Boss and Eurocos. Frankfurt, Germany. 5ml (.17oz.) A woody fragrance.

JOSEPH ABBOUD eau de toilette pour homme by Euroitalia. Monza, Italy. The 5ml (.16oz.) amber glass bottle has "SGD" molded into the bottom.

BRUT 33 splash-on lotion for men by Faberge, Inc. NY, NY. 15ml (1/2oz.).

REGATTA aftershave for men by The Fuller Brush Co. Hartford CT. 3.75ml (1/8oz.).

L'UOMO GHERARDINI eau de toilette pour homme by Parfums Gherardini. Firenze, Italy. 6ml (1/5oz.). "GHERARDINI FIRENZE" is molded into the bottom of the bottle and a filled-in "G" is part of the front and back mold.

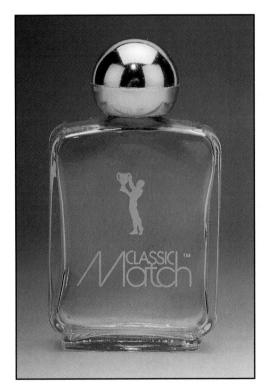

CLASSIC MATCH version of GIORGIO for men by Giorgio Beverly Hills. Beverly Hills, CA. A division of Belcam Inc. Rosses Point, NY. 15ml (1/2oz.).

GIORGIO eau de toilette for men by
Giorgio Beverly Hills. Beverly Hills, CA.
3.5ml (1/8oz.).

INSENSE eau de toilette pour homme by Parfums Givenchy. The 7ml
(1/4oz.) bottle has "HP" molded into the bottom.

HALSTON 1-12 cologne for men by Halston Fragrances, Inc. NY, NY. 15ml
(1/2oz.). The squeezed brown glass bottle contains a citrus fragrance.

GUCCI cologne pour homme by Gucci. Paris, France. The 7.5ml
(1/4oz.) glass bottle has a gold cap with green and red stripes.

RUSSIAN LEATHER aftershave lotion for men by Imperial Del Oro. Long Beach, CA. The gold-splotched bottle holds 15ml (1/2oz.).

HALSTON LIMITED cologne for men by Halston Fragrances, Inc. NY, NY. A 7.5ml (1/4oz.) purple glass bottle.

SERGIO SOLDANO eau de toilette for men by Intercosma. Genoa, Italy. A 6ml (.2oz.) plastic-encased bottle.

JOOP! NIGHT FLIGHT eau de toilette pour homme by Parfums Joop! Paris, France. The 7.5ml (1/4oz.) blue glass bottle is decorated with night stars.

MAN BY JOVAN cologne for men by Jovan. A
green tinted fragrance with a brown stopper in a
15ml (1/2oz.) bottle.

LENEL cologne for men by Lenel Parfums
Inc. Distributed by Frances Rothschild, Inc.
Dallas, TX. NY, NY. 3.75ml (1/8oz.)

HAWK cologne for men by The Mennen
Co. Morristown, NJ. 7.5ml (1/4oz.)

MONTANA aftershave lotion pour homme by
Claude Montana Parfums. Paris, France. The grey
plastic case opens to the 4ml (.13oz.) round bottle.

Below: SERGIO TACCHINI eau de toilette by Sergio Tacchini. Italy. Distributed by Morris. 7.5ml (1/4oz.).

PHOTO eau de toilette pour homme by Parfums Lagerfeld and Parfums International Ltd. NY, NY. 15ml (1/2oz.) A citrus fragrance.

LIMOUSINE eau de toilette limited edition pour homme by Parlux Fragrances, Inc. Paris, France. Distributed from Old Tappan, NJ. 5ml (.17oz.)

PHANTOM eau de toilette pour homme by Parlux Fragrances, Inc. Paris, France. 5ml (.17oz.). Inspired by "The Phantom of the Opera."

MINOTAURE eau de toilette pour homme by Parfums Paloma Picasso. Paris, France. Distributed by Cosmair Inc. NY, NY. The 5ml (1/6oz.) frosted bottle has "MINOTAURE" in raised letters. A woody fragrance.

CEDRAT eau de toilette pour homme by Ed Pinaud. Paris, France. The black 4ml (.13oz.) bottle has "BOTTLE MADE IN FRANCE, H" molded into the bottom.

MEDITERRANEUM eau de toilette pour homme by Proteo. Italy. 7.5ml (1/4oz.).

ROMEO GIGLI eau de toilette pour uomo by Proteo. Italy. The 5ml (.17oz.) glass bottle has "ROMEO GIGLI" molded into the bottom and the neck is wrapped in wire with a violet stopper.

X S excess pour homme eau de toilette by Parfums Paco Rabanne. Paris, France. 3.75ml (1/8oz.). The fragrance was introduced in 1993.

PUB cologne for men by Revlon. NY, NY. A brown glass 15ml (1/2oz.) bottle.

BIGARADE bracing body splash pour homme by Parfums Nina Ricci. Paris, France. The fragrance, introduced in 1971, is contained in a bottle designed by Marc Lalique. 15ml (1/2oz.). "BOTTLE MADE IN FRANCE" is molded into the bottom.

PANCALDI eau de toilette pour homme by Rivara Division Honorah and Diana de Silva Cosmetics. Milan, Italy. A beautiful soft black 5ml (.17oz.) bottle.

GLOBE eau de toilette pour homme by Parfums Rochas. Paris, France. The beautiful bottle has the "HP" trademark molded into the bottom. 15ml (1/2oz.).

MONSIEUR ROCHAS eau de cologne pour homme by Parfums Rochas. Paris, France. 3.75ml (1/8oz.).

OPEN eau de toilette pour homme by Roger & Gallet. Paris, France. 7ml (.24oz.).

EXOTIC MUSK for men de Rothschild Ltd. Shown with AMBER cologne for men by Frances Rothschild, Inc. Dallas, TX and NY, NY. 3.75ml (1/8oz.).

DE ROTHSCHILD eau de toilette, a man's fragrance by Frances Rothschild, Inc. Dallas, TX. NY, NY. 3.75ml (1/8oz.).

MEN'S CLUB eau de toilette by Parfums Helena Rubinstein Men's Division. NY, NY; Paris, France; London, England; Dusseldorf, Germany. 3.75ml (1/8oz.).

JIL SANDER FEELING MAN eau de toilette by Jil Sander. Wiesbaden, Germany. 7.5ml (1/4oz.).

LACOSTE eau de toilette pour homme by Sofipar International Inc. Paris, France. The 4ml (.14oz.) green glass bottle has "SGD" molded into the bottom.

BRITISH STERLING cologne for men. Distributed by Speidel. Providence, RI. 3.75ml (1/8oz.).

VAN GILS eau de toilette pour homme by Van Gils Cosmetics. Paris, France. 10ml (1/3oz.).

CASAQUE eau de toilette pour homme by Parfums Jean-Louis Vermeil. Paris, France. The green horseshoe bottle holds 10ml (1/3oz.).

ZEGNA eau de toilette pour homme by Ermenegildo Zegna, Italy. Distributed by Antonio Puig. Barcelona Spain. The bottle has the "HP" trademark on the bottom. The box is marked 7ml (.6oz.) It's .24oz. (not .6oz.)

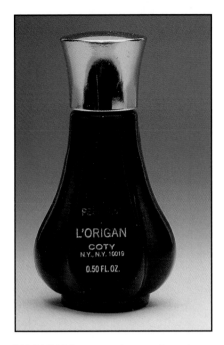

L'ORIGAN creamy skin perfume by Coty, Inc. NY, NY. The black bottle has gold lettering and a gold cap, and holds 15ml (1/2oz.) L'ORIGAN was introduced in 1909.

CHANTILLY liquid skin sachet by Houbigant. Paris, France and NY, NY. 15ml (1/2oz.) The company explained to customers that "liquid skin sachet is a new perfume medium, originated by Houbigant."

CHANTILLY sachet by Houbigant. NY, NY. 1-2/5oz.) The bottle contains a pink talc sachet. A white cap and a pink bow.

APRIL SHOWERS sachet by Cheramy. NY, NY. 5/7oz. The powder form contains a high percentage of fragrant oil in a silky pressed powder.

VIOLET SEC sachet and YANKY CLOVER sachet by Richard Hudnut. Paris, France. NY, NY. 1.25oz. bottles.

BLUE CARNATION sachet (1/2oz.) and VIOLETTE DE PARME sachet (3/4oz.) dry perfume by Roger & Gallet. NY, NY.

APRIL VIOLETS sachet by Yardley. London, England. Distributed in the U.S.A. by Yardley. NY, NY. The Bakelite cap has a bee as part of its design, and covers the sealed 30ml (1oz.) bottle from the 1950s. "YARDLEY, LONDON" is molded into the bottom of the bottle.

TWEED talc by Lentheric Perfumes. Paris, France; Chicago, IL; London, England; NY, NY. The 3/4oz. tin can with a wood cover has "CONTAINER MADE IN ENGLAND" printed on the bottom.

Left: VIOLET talc powder by the J.B. Williams Co. Glastonbury, CT. 1/2oz. Printed on the back of the can: "Guaranteed under the United States Food and Drug Act of June 30, 1906. Ser. No. 3715." The brass cap is hinged. The can is from the late teens or early 1920s.

DeVilbiss perfume atomizers. Called "Perfumizers" by the Devilbiss Co. Toledo, OH. The Devilbiss Co. produced atomizers until 1969. "DEVILBISS, MADE IN U.S.A." is molded into the bottom of the bottles.

DeVilbiss pump atomizers by the Devilbiss Co. Toledo, OH. Two beautiful china atomizers.

Miniature atomizer with a funnel.

Two hand-blown glass bottles. The pig has a NARZISSE perfume label and is from Germany. Similar animal-shaped bottles were popular from the early 1900s through the 1930s. The round bottle has a glass dauber.

AFTER FIVE solid perfume pendant by Auvergne et Cie, Inc. East Longmeadow, MA. 3ml (.09oz.). The fragrance was introduced in 1937.

Five beautiful hand-decorated glass bottles. The flowers are made of painted sea shells. Four of the bottles are 3.75ml (1/8oz.) and one is 7.5ml (1/4oz.).

Never choose a fragrance because it smells good on someone else; everyone's body chemistry is different.

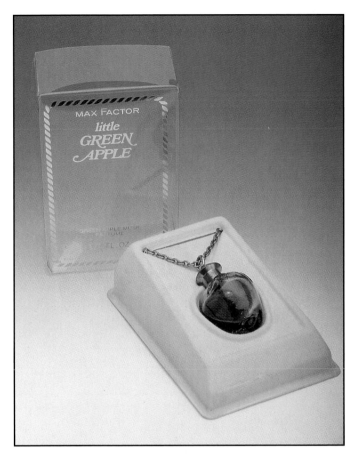

Left: LITTLE GREEN APPLE perfume by Max Factor. Hollywood, CA; London, England; Paris, France. 3.75ml (1/8oz.). The apple bottle-pendant is made of green glass and hangs on a gold-plated chain. From the 1960s.

Right: A black glass pendant bottle with a pouch and a plastic pump for filling the 7.5ml (1/4oz.) bottle.

A gold-cased solid perfume pendant with a jade center stone.

A beautiful solid perfume brooch.

A needlepoint flower on a white background, overlaid on a gold-encased 3.75ml (1/8oz.) bottle with a glass dauber. The bottle is a bar pin.

Tompadouc Viennese Handicraft made in Austria. 7.5ml (1/4oz.). The flat, round bottle has a circle molded into its clear glass, on both front and back. It has a plastic circle with a needlepoint flower in the center that is glued on the front. The bottle, topped with a gold metal cap with a glass dauber, comes in a clear case.

Needlepoint rose pattern on black. The glass bottles with glass daubers hold 3.75ml (1/8oz.) and 7.5ml (1/4oz.).

A brass bottle with a brass cap attached by a chain. Jeweled and painted, with a circle of beautiful flowers detailed in colored stone inlay. Very Victorian. "MADE IN FRANCE" is stamped on the neck of the bottle.

A Czechoslovakian bottle. Gilt gold filigree overlays the amber-colored glass bottle, which has a glass dauber. Rhinestone jewels adorn the leaf design. The tag on the neck has "Czechoslovakia" stamped into it.

This popular purse flacon has sterling silver overlay on a 3.75ml (1/8oz.) bottle. "HENCO IN MEXICO, DP" is stamped into the bottom.

A gilded 3ml (.10oz.) glass bottle with a pink cord, formed to resemble a rose flower.

A 7.5ml (1/4oz.) glass bottle that has been decorated with a plastic flower on the brass cap and a ballerina on the front.

A 7.5ml (1/4oz.) glass purse flacon with a red rose cap. A popular dime store bottle.

Boutique purse flacon. The 1 dram bottle is gold-plated with mother of pearl inlay. It is boxed with a plastic funnel.

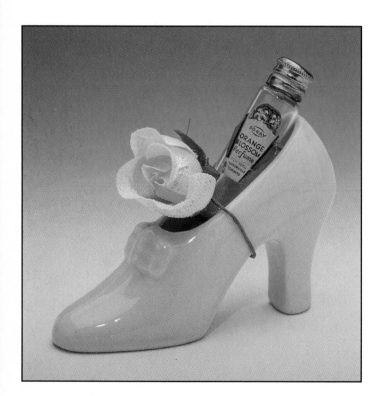

ORANGE BLOSSOM perfume by Bo-Kay Perfumer. NY, NY; Jacksonville, FL; Toronto, ON. The 3ml (.1oz.) vial has a brass cap and is held in a porcelain shoe.

FLORALE parfum by Robinson Cosmetics Co. Inc. NY, NY. The half-dram bottle is part of the old-fashioned telephone. It came painted in pink, blue, red, and green. A dime store novelty from the early 1950s.

GALA NIGHT fragrance by Bouton. NY, NY. A 3ml (.10oz.) hurricane candle bottle.

Hurricane oil lamp from the early 1950s. The ruby glass bottle has a brass cap and holder and a ruby chimney. 3.75ml (1/8oz.). It contained an unknown fragrance.

Perfume Hi-lights by Stuart Products Co. St. Paul, MN. The company was founded by William B. Cohen in 1935. The chain pulls the tray down for access to the three half-dram bottles. The brass and glass floor lamp was introduced in 1939. Slightly different patterns were used by the different contract manufactures.

CABBAGE PATCH KIDS perfume by Original Appalachian Artworks, Inc. The 15ml (1/2oz.) bottle is from 1983.

Left: BOUQUET perfume by Lander Co. Inc. NY, NY. A seasonal 15ml (1/2oz.) bottle.

Right: HEAVEN perfume by Lander Co. Inc. NY, NY. The fragrance is in a candle-shaped bottle, and the plastic cap is shaped like a red flame. APPLE BLOSSOM perfume by Lander Co. Inc. The 3.75ml (1/8oz.) candle bottle is part of the angel figurine.

Sophisti-Cats by Max Factor. Hollywood, CA; London, England; Paris, France. The cats are holding GOLDEN WOODS and HYPNOTIQUE perfumes introduced in 1951. 3.75ml (1/8oz.). They are from the 1960s.

Avon

Avon Products Incorporated has steadily grown since its beginning as the California Perfume Company, which was established in 1886. The famous phrase, "Avon Calling," is known throughout the world as a distinctive guarantee of high quality cosmetics and toiletry items for the entire family, conveniently brought to the home by an Avon representative.

The firm's foundation of success is based on *quality:* quality products, quality service and quality relationships with customers. It is the largest manufacturer and distributor of cosmetics, fragrances and costume jewelry in the world.

Avon bottles still holds interest for many collectors. The company is distributing beautiful new miniature fragrances that are worthy additions to any collection.

For a more detailed history on Avon, see my book, *Miniature Perfume Bottles.* Also, a source of updated information can be found in Bud Hastins' book, *Avon & California Perfume Company Collector's Encyclopedia,* 14th Edition.

CASBAH eau de toilette by Avon Products, Inc. NY, NY. This deluxe petite blue glass bottle was made by Parfums Creatifs. Paris, France. 4ml (.13oz.). 1994.

FAR AWAY parfum by Avon Products, Inc. NY, NY. 4ml (.125oz.). 1994.

C'EST MOI! eau de toilette by Avon Products, Inc. NY, NY. A deluxe petite by Parfum Creatifs. Paris, France. 4ml (.13oz.). 1994.

Left: PERLE NOIRE eau de toilette by Avon Products, Inc. NY, NY. A deluxe petite by Parfum Creatifs. Paris, France. 4ml (.13oz.). 1994.

LAHANA perfume by
Avon Products, Inc. NY,
NY. 4ml (.125oz.). 1995.

NATORI perfume
by Avon Products,
Inc. NY, NY. 4ml
(.13oz.). 1995.

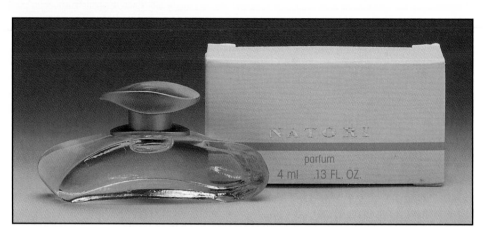

VANILLA soft musk cologne by Avon Products, Inc. NY, NY. 4ml
(.125oz.). 1995.

NIGHT MAGIC evening musk perfume by Avon
Products, Inc. NY, NY. 4ml (.125oz.). 1995.

Parisian Garden by Avon Products, Inc. NY, NY. The 10ml (.33oz.) white milk glass bottle contained CHARISMA, MOONWIND, or SONNET perfume. 1974-1975.

Perfume Flaconette of 1923 by The California Perfume Co. Inc. NY, NY. The octagonal-shaped bottle contained TRAILING ARBUTUS. The brass cap has "California Perfume Company" stamped into it. The label is wrapped around the neck.

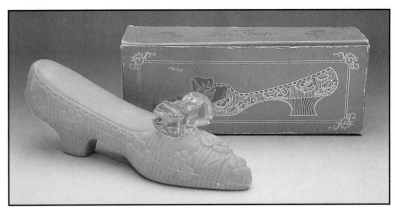

Lady Slipper by Avon Products, Inc. NY, NY. The 3.75ml (1/8oz.) bow-shaped bottle containing COTILLION tops the pink perfumed soap slipper. CHARISMA and COTILLION were the fragrances used in this 1970 item.

TOPAZE perfume by The California Perfume Co. Inc. Avon Products, Inc. Division. NY, NY and Montreal, Canada. The fragrance in this bottle was introduced to celebrate the 50th wedding anniversary of Mr. and Mrs. D.H. McConnell, founders of the California Perfume Company. This bottle was offered only in 1935 and sold new for 20 cents. 7.5ml (1/4oz.).

TRAILING ARBUTUS eau de cologne by Avon California Perfume Co., Avon Products, Inc. NY, NY. A 1978 Anniversary Keepsake. 45ml (1.5oz.).

AVON FOR MEN. Men's Aftershave Samples by Avon Products, Inc. NY, NY. The box, in a red woven design, contains eight bottles, each 3.75ml (1/8oz.). From 1973. The samples contain AVON LEATHER (1966), BRAVO (1969), DEEP WOODS (1972), OLAND (1970), SPICY (1965), TAI WINDS (1971), TRIBUTE (1963), WINDJAMMER (1973).

AVON FRAGRANCES Demonstrator No 1. "Whatever you wear — wear fragrances from Avon Products, Inc." NY, NY. The box, in a blue woven design, contains fourteen bottles, each 3.75ml (1/8oz.). From (1973). The samples contain BIRD OF PARADISE (1970), CHARISMA (1968), COTILLION (1937), FIELD FLOWERS (1970), HERE'S MY HEART (1958), IMPERIAL GARDEN (1973), MOONWIND (1971), OCCUR! (1963), PATCHWORK (1972), ROSES, ROSES (1972), SONNET (1941), TO A WILD ROSE (1950), TOPAZE (1935), UNFORGETTABLE (1965).

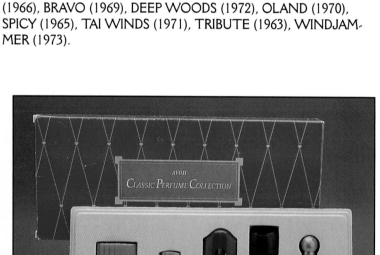

Avon Classic Perfume Collection by Avon Products, Inc. NY, NY. The 1995 set, introduced in 1994, contains five deluxe miniature collectibles: SOFTMUSK, LAHANA, IMARI, NIGHT MAGIC, and MESMERIZE perfumes in 4ml (.125oz.) bottles.

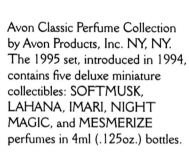

Colgate's Miniature Size Extracts by Colgate & Company. NY, NY. The extracts are in 1 dram glass bottles with brass caps. A circled "C&CO" is molded into the bottom of the bottle. The fragrances are CAPRICE, CASHMERE BOUQUET (1869), DACTYLIS (1901), LA FRANCE ROSE (1922), and MONAD VIOLET (1901). The set was sold, shipped and billed by C.H. Selick, Inc. Perfumers, 56 Leonard Street, NY, NY, in 1920.

Miniature Perfumes by Colgate & Company. NY, NY. The three 1 dram bottles contain the following Colgate's extracts: CASHMERE BOUQUET (1869), DACTYLIS (1901), and LA FRANCE ROSE (1922), all in the original box. The set is from the late 1920s.

Flowers of the Evening tote set by The House of Martens. NY, NY. The locked set contains GARDENIA, LAVENDER, and VIOLET in 7.5ml (1/4oz.) bottles. The set is from the late 1920s.

Book of Perfume by Cardinal. NY, NY. The beautiful set opens to three book bottles containing GARDENIA, BOUQUET, and CHYPRE perfume. 7.5ml (1/4oz.) The set was introduced in 1939.

Duvinne of NY, NY. This set features CARNATION, GARDENIA, and LILAC perfumes in a round glass ball container. The top half is clear; the bottom half is painted and holds a metal tray with three jewel-topped, brass-capped bottles, each 3.75ml (1/8oz.). From the early 1940s.

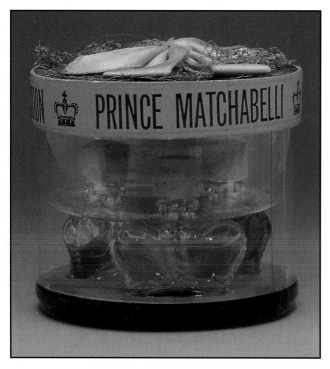

Perfume Collection by Prince Matchabelli, Inc. NY, NY. The three-bottle set comes in a round plastic case and contains half-dram bottles of CROWN JEWEL (1945), STRADIVARI (1950), and WIND SONG (1953). The set is from the late 1950s.

Ivel Perfumes by Ivel. NY, NY. The three-bottle set contains CHYPRE, GARDENIA, and MON DESIR in 7.5ml (1/4oz.) bottles.

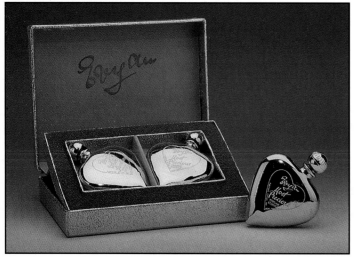

Left: Evyan's Two Golden Hearts set by Evyan. NY, NY. The two 3.75ml (1/8oz.) gilded heart-shaped bottles contain perfume essences of MOST PRECIOUS (1947) and WHITE SHOULDERS (1943). The set is from the late 1950s.

Below: Perfumed writing sets by Chanel. Paris, France. The sets contain ballpoint pens in a 14 kt. gold, exclusive design. The scents ARPEGE and CHANEL NO 5 are mixed into the ink. A CHANEL NO 5 dummy or factice is shown in the background.

EXQUISIT 750 by Gerard. Paris, France. The set is from the late 1960s, and contains the following fragrances in 2 gram or 1.87ml (1/16oz.) bottles: VIVARA parfum by Emilio Pucci, 1966; CABOCHARD parfum by Parfums Gres, 1959; PARCE QUE parfum by Parfums Capucci, 1963; JOILE MADAME parfum by Parfums Balmain, 1953; and CALYPSO parfum by Robert Piguet, 1960.

Cosmopolitan's Collection of Internationally Famous Perfumes. Distributed from NY, NY. The ten-bottle set contains the following fragrances: INTOXICATION by D'Orsay, ODALISQUE by Nettie Rosenstein, CAPRICCI by Nina Ricci, FAME by Parfums Corday, CARNEGIE PINK by Hattie Carnegie, L'AIR DU TEMPS by Nina Ricci, BANDIT by Robert Piguet, FLUER SAUVAGE by Germaine Monteil, PROPHECY by Prince Matchabelli, and JUNGLE GARDENIA by Tuvache.

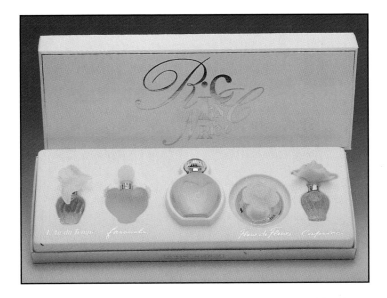

A Nina Ricci set from the 1980s. The set contains five of Nina's fragrances in beautiful Lalique bottles: L'AIR DU TEMPS (3.5ml or .12oz.), FAROUCHE (3.5ml or .12oz.), NINA (4.75ml or .16oz.), FLEUR DE FLEURS (3.5ml or .12oz.), and CAPRICCI (3.5ml or .12oz.).

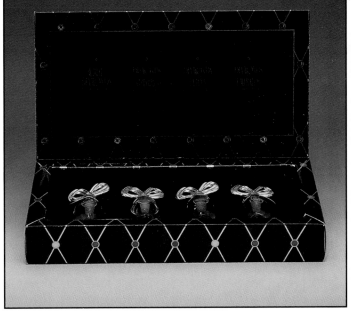

Elizabeth Taylor's Fragrant Jewel Collection of fragrances introduced in 1993. The set is by Parfum International, Ltd. NY, NY, and consists of 3.75ml (1/8oz.) bottles: DIAMONDS AND EMERALDS parfum, a floral fragrance; DIAMONDS AND RUBIES parfum, a floral-oriental fragrance; DIAMONDS AND SAPPHIRES eau de toilette, a floral-fruity fragrance; and WHITE DIAMONDS parfum, a floral fragrance from 1991.

Right: Estee Lauder "FRAGRANCE TREASURES" by Estee Lauder. NY, NY. The 1993 set contains ten of Estee's fragrances: WHITE LINEN, a floral-aldehyde perfume, 1978, 2.6ml (.09oz.); KNOWING, a chypre-floral parfum, 1988, 3.5ml (.12oz.); CINNABAR, an oriental-spicy perfume, 1978, 3.5ml (.12oz.); BEAUTIFUL, a floral perfume, 1985, 3.5ml (.12oz.); SPELLBOUND, a floral-ambery perfume, 1991, 3.5ml (.12oz.); ESTEE, a floral perfume, 1968, 3.5ml (.12oz.); PRIVATE COLLECTION, a chypre-green perfume, 1973, 1.9ml (.07oz.); YOUTH-DEW, an oriental-ambery spicy perfume, 1953, 3.5ml (.12oz.); AZUREE, a chypre-floral animalic fragrance, 1969, 3.5ml (.12oz.); and ALIAGE, a chypre-green fragrance, 1972, 4.6ml (.15oz.).

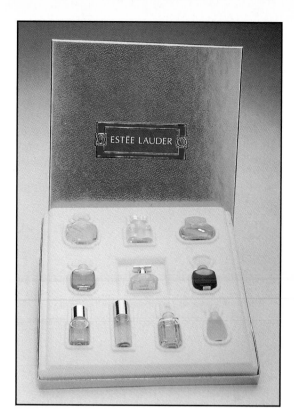

Left: Estee Lauder "SMALL WONDERS" by Estee Lauder. NY, NY. The 1994 set contains five of Estee's fragrances: BEAUTIFUL perfume, 3.5ml (.12oz.); WHITE LINEN perfume, 2.6ml (.09oz.); KNOWING parfum, 3.5ml (.12oz.); YOUTH-DEW perfume, 3.5ml (.12oz.); and SPELLBOUND perfume, 3.5ml (.12oz.).

Miniature perfume bottles are beautifully displayed on a mirror. This mirror is framed by an abalone inlay design. Use your imagination when displaying your minis!

Perfume Information & Guidelines

Over the centuries, fragrances have been prepared in many different forms. Today, liquid scents are described by a variety of terms, each indicating a different strength. From strongest to most diluted (with the average fragrance concentration noted), they are as follows:

1. Parfum or perfume (15% to 30%)
2. Eau de parfum (8% to 15%)
3. Parfum de toilette (6% to 12%)
4. Eau de toilette (4% to 8%)
5. Eau de cologne (2% to 5%)
6. Cologne (1% to 3%)
7. Toilet water (1% to 2%)

Parfum or *perfume* is a volatile liquid which can be distilled from flowers or prepared synthetically. Because perfume contains more fragrance and oil than other scented preparations, it has the highest fragrance strength value and lasts the longest. This makes it the most expensive of all preparations.

Fragrances with prefixes such as "eau" (meaning water) contain a certain amount of distilled water mixed with the alcohol, along with the fragrance concentrate. *Eau de parfum, eau de toilet,* and *eau de cologne* are in this descriptive category.

Parfum de toilette contains a substantial amount of fragrance concentrate that is diluted with alcohol.

Cologne is a scented liquid consisting of a variety of fragrant oils in lesser amounts than in perfume, diluted with more alcohol. The word is a French derivation of "Koln," the city in western Germany where cologne has been made since the eighteenth century. The original cologne, 4711, was named for the street address of the parfum house that manufactured it in Koln, Germany.

Toilet water is a scented liquid with a high alcohol content. It is used in bathing, after shaving, or as a skin freshner.

FRAGRANCE ABBREVIATIONS

PARF = parfum
PERF = perfume
EDP = eau de parfum
PDT = parfum de toilette
EDT = eau de toilette
EDC = eau de cologne
COL = cologne
TW = toilet water

Families of Scents

The numerous varities of perfumes have been classified into basic scent types in order to provide a guideline when choosing fragrances.

CHYPRE is a strong, spicy scent that is a blend of citrus, oakmoss, patchouli, and sandalwood. The word "Chypre" is traced to Francois Coty, who created Chypre perfume while on the Island of Cyprus.

CITRUS is a clean, tangy scent that is blended with oils of bergamot, lemon, lime, tangerine and bitter orange blossoms.

FLORALS are usually a clean, sweet-smelling scent, with multi-blends of many individual floral bouquets. The largest number of fragrances are in this category.

FOUGERE is the French word for fern and has a fresh woodland scent. Fougere fragrances have no fern odor, but depend on aromatic chemicals to produce the interpretation of fern-like notes. It is a term used to describe a blend of lavender, oakmoss and coumarin, (a synthetic that smells like hay.)

FRUITY blends are clean, fresh-fruit scents with blends of lemons and oranges, with a peach-like warmth.

GREEN is usually the top note of a fragrance composition that has a strong scent of fresh-cut grass and green leaves, made from the blends of grass, juniper, leaves and pine.

MODERN BLENDS or ALDEHYDES are entirely new fragrant scents that are not found in nature, they are created individually by the parfumer's imagination. Aldehyde is an organic chemical that contains a useful group of a carbon, a hydrogen and an oxygen atom. They are derived from natural or synthetic materials and usually have a rich top note.

ORIENTAL BLENDS are in the heavy category with warm scents of spices, musk, resins, exotic flowers and balsam.

SPICY is a strong, sweet scent that contains blends of actual spices such as cardamon, cinnamon, cloves. Flowers with spicy notes such as carnation and lavender are also blended.

WOODY-MOSSY is a clean, crisp, foresty scent that contains blends of cedar, rosewood, sandalwood and other aromatic woods that are combined with oakmoss and ferns.

Sub-Categories

Fragrances are also divided into sub-combinations in order to define the variations.

FLORAL-GREEN is a combined scent of sweet-smelling floral with green notes of crisp leaves and fresh-cut grass.

FLORAL-FRUITY is a blend of floral bouquets with fresh-fruit scents.

FLORAL-FRESH is a light, spring floral scent with citrus blends that add a powdery touch.

FLORAL-ALDEHYDES usually have a strong and rich top note of floral blends that represent a new fragrant scent not found in nature, that consists of natural or synthetic materials.

FLORAL-AMBERY combines a rich floral blend with the soft powdery qualities of amber and creates a sweet, warm scent.

FLORAL-ORIENTAL is a blend of exotic florals with warm, heavy scents of spices, musk, balsam and resin.

ORIENTAL-AMBERY is a blend of fresh citrus with the soft powdery essence of amber and a hint of vanilla.

ORIENTAL-SPICY is a heavy scent of spices, in addition to spicy florals, musk and dry woods.

CHYPRE-FRUITY is a combined blend of the peach with strong woodsy traces that creates a warm, mellow fragrance.

CHYPRE-FLORAL ANIMALIC is a combined blend of woodsy traces, along with florals and sensual animalic base notes. Animal-like ingredients such as ambergris, civet, musk and castoreum are usually synthetic reproductions.

CHYPRE-FLORAL is a light blend of rich florals, along with citrus, oakmoss and patchouli.

CHYPRE-FRESH is a combined blend of woodsy scents that are enhanced by a fresh citrus blend.

CHYPRE-GREEN is a blend of woodsy scents, along with the strong scent of grass, leaves and aromatic woods, that creates a strong forest scent.

Bibliography

Ball, Joanne Dubbs and Torem, Dorothy Hehl. *Commercial Fragrance Bottles.* Pennsylvania, Schiffer Publishing, Ltd., 1993.

Barille, Elisabeth and Laroze, Catherine. *The Book of Perfume.* Paris and New York, Flammarion, 1995.

Hastin, Bud. *Avon & California Perfume Company Collector's Encyclopedia.* 14th Edition. Published, written, photographed and researched by Bud Hastin. Missouri, 1995.

Hastin, Bud. *Avon Bottle Encycolpedia.* Written and produced by Bud Hastin. Missouri, Reliance Printing Company, 1974.

Lefkowith, Christie Mayer. *The Art of Perfume.* New York, Thames & Hudson Inc., 1994.

Moran, Jan. *Fabulous Fragrances.* California, Crescent House Publishing, 1994.

North, Jacquelyne Y. Jones. *Commercial Perfume Bottles.* Pennsylvania, Schiffer Publishing, Ltd., 1987.

North, Jacquelyne Y. Jones. *Perfume, Cologne and Scent Bottles.* Pennsylvania, Schiffer Publishing, Ltd., 1986.

The Fragrance Foundation. *The History, The Mystery, The Enjoyment of Fragrance.* New York, The Fragrance Foundation. Founded 1949.

Utt, Glenn and Mary Lou with Bayer, Patricia. *Lalique Perfume Bottles.* New York, Crown Publishers Inc., 1985.

Price Reference

This price reference is intended to be a guide only. Because the marketplace is constantly changing, prices may be lower or higher than stated herein. These prices have been found in the geographical area to which the author has access. Many factors determine the price, including the size and condition of the bottle, whether the bottle is full or empty, and if the fragrance has its original box.

Fragrance	Bottle size	Price (U.S.$)

Fragrance	Bottle size	Price	Fragrance	Bottle size	Price	Fragrance	Bottle size	Price
1000	.23oz.	75	ASJA	.17oz.	11	BOUQUET SUPREME	1/8oz.	8
1800	1/16oz.	6	AVIANCE	1/8oz.	8	BOURRASQUE	1/32oz.	50
360	1/8oz.	17	AVIANCE NIGHT MUSK	1/4oz.	8	BREATHLESS	1/4oz.	10
8e JOUR	1/4oz.	12	AZURRE	.12oz.	12	BRITISH STERLING		
A V	1/4oz.	12	BAHAMOUR	1oz.	50	for men	1/8oz.	5
ABANO	1/16oz.	8	BAKIR	1/2oz.	10	BRUT 33 for men	1/2oz.	5
ABANO scepter	1/4oz.	10	BANDIT	1/4oz.	15	C K ONE	1/16oz.	5
ADVENTURE	.27oz.	10	BARYNIA	.17oz.	13	C'EST LA VIE!	.13oz.	16
ALIAGE	1/8oz.	6	BAVARDAGE	1/16oz.	8	CABOCHARD	.1oz.	15
ALIAGE	.15oz.	12	BEETHOVEN for men	1/3oz.	10	CABOCHARD	1/16oz.	12
ALINE	.2oz.	7	BELLODGIA	1/2oz.	20	CABOTINE	.1oz.	20
ALORS	1/4oz.	15	BELLODGIA	1/4oz.	20	CABRIOLE	1/8oz.	8
ALURIA	1/8oz.	50	BELOVED	1/16oz.	6	CACHET	1/8oz.	8
AMBER for men	1/8oz.	4	BEN HUR	1/8oz.	25		1/4oz.	6
AMBRE IRISE VERT	1/16oz.	5/ea.	BEN HUR	1/4oz.	12	CALVIN KLEIN	1/4oz.	8
ANGEL	.14oz.	25	BENDELILAS	1/2oz.	35	CALYPSO	1/16oz.	10
APPLE BLOSSOM			BIAGIOTTI UOMO			CANOE for men	1/8oz.	5
by C.H. Selick	1/2oz.	75	for men	.17oz.	8	CAPRICCI	1/16oz.	75
APPLE BLOSSOM			BIBI	.24oz.	10	CAPRICCI	1/4oz.	20
by Fuller Brush	1/8oz.	7	BIGARADE for men	1/2oz.	15	CARDIN	1/8oz.	8
APPLE BLOSSOM			BLAZER	1/2oz.	8	CARLO CORINTO ROUGE		
by Lander	1/4oz.	10	BLUE CARNATION sachet	1/2oz.	5	for men	1/3oz.	11
APRIL SHOWERS	1/2oz.	12	BLUE GRASS	.2oz.	8	CARNEGIE PINK	1/16oz.	10
APRIL SHOWERS sachet	5/7oz.	5	BLUE GRASS	1/4oz.	12	CASAQUE	1/16oz.	12
APRIL VIOLETS sachet	1oz.	5	BLUE WALTZ	5/8oz.	20	CASAQUE for men	1/3oz.	8
ARAMIS 900 for men	1/4oz.	5	BLUE WALTZ	1/4oz.	35	CATALYST	.125oz.	14
ARAMIS for men	1/2oz.	9	BOIS DE VETIVER for men	1/8oz.	5	CEDRAT for men	.13oz.	5
ARMANI for men	.17oz.	5	BONJOUR	1/4oz.	7	CHALEUR	1/2oz.	7
ARPEGE	.17oz.	10	BOSS for men	.17oz.	6	CHAMADE	1/16oz.	13
ARPEGE	1/4oz.	15	BOUQUET	1/8oz.	15	CHAMADE	1/6oz.	20

Name	Size	Price
	1/2oz.	40
CHAMPAGNE		
by Germaine Monteil	.19oz.	12
CHAMPAGNE by YSL	.26oz.	25
CHANEL NO 5	1/4oz.	25
CHANEL NO 5	.13oz.	12
CHANTEL	1/2oz.	8
CHANTILLY	1/8oz.	8
CHANTILLY		
liquid skin sachet	1/2oz.	6
CHANTILLY sachet	1-2/5oz.	5
CHARMANTE	1/2oz.	10
CHEN YU		
FLOWERING ALMOND	1/8oz.	8
CHERISH	1/8oz.	10
CHESS PIECES	3/32oz.	5/ea.
CHLOE	.12oz.	15
CHYPRE	1/2oz.	12
CINNABAR	.22oz.	15
CINNABAR	.12oz.	20
CITANA	.08oz.	8
CLAIBORNE for men	1/2oz.	10
CLASSIC MATCH for men	1/2oz.	5
COCKTAIL DRY	.1oz.	15
COCO	1/16oz.	12
COEUR DE CANANGA	1/15oz.	5
COEUR JOIE	1/4oz.	20
CONCRETA MUGUET	1/16oz.	10
CONFETTI	1/16oz.	10
CONFETTI	1/8oz.	25
CORDON D'OR	1/8oz.	10
Coty bottle for		
LIPAS POURPRE	1/4oz.	25
Coty bottles	20oz.	5
	30oz.	8
	40oz.	8
COURANT	1/2oz.	10
CREDO	1/4oz.	10
CROYANCE	1/4oz.	10
DALINI	1/4oz.	25
DANCE ARROGANCE	.16oz.	18
DE ROTHSCHILD for men	1/8oz.	6
DEBONAIR for men	1/8oz.	5
DECOLLETE	.14oz.	10
DELICIOUS	.1oz.	13
DESERT FLOWER	1/16oz.	10
DESIGN	1/4oz.	25
DESIRADE	.14oz.	14
DESIRE	.85 dram.	
	31oz.	10/ea.
DETCHEMA	1/16oz.	12
DIAMONDS AND RUBIES	.17oz.	8
DIORESSENCE	1/4oz.	11
DIVINE	1/6oz.	16
DNA	.16oz.	12
DNA	.07oz.	5
DOLCE & GABBANA	.16oz.	18
DONNA	1/5oz.	9
DuBe bottle	1/4oz.	8
DUNHILL for men	.16oz.	9
EAU DE CHARLOTTE	.26oz.	13
EAU DE ROCHAS	.34oz.	9
EGOISTE PLATINUM		
for men	.13oz.	9
ELLIPSE	1/8oz.	15
ELYSIUM	.17oz.	25
EMERAUDE	1/4oz.	16
EMERAUDE	1/2oz.	10
EMERAUDE brass encased	1/8oz.	20
EMIR	.1oz.	20
EMOTION	1/4oz.	7
EMPREINTE	1/8oz.	15
ENGLISH SPICE	1/2oz.	10
ENIGMA	.12oz.	8
EPRIS	.12oz.	20
ESTEE	.12oz.	17
ETERNITY	.13oz.	20
EVENING IN PARIS	.15oz.	12
EVENING IN PARIS	1/8oz.	10/ea.
EVENING IN PARIS		
gold cap	1/4oz.	10
EVENING IN PARIS		
tasseled cap	1/4oz.	25/ea.
EVENING IN PARIS		
white cap	1/4oz.	12
EXOTIC MUSK for men	1/8oz.	4
EXPRESSION	1/8oz.	12
EXTRA	1/8oz.	20
FABERGE flambeau	vial	15
FAME	1/16oz.	10
FANTASIA	1/8oz.	15
FANTASME	.15oz.	11
FAROUCHE	.1oz.	30
FAROUCHE	1/3oz.	20
FASHION	1/16oz.	5
FATH DE FATH	1/8oz.	12
FEMINA	1/4oz.	14
FINESSE	1/2oz.	7
FIORILU	.13oz.	14
FIORILU on leaf	.13oz.	20
FLAMBEAU	1/2oz.	12
FLAME	1/16oz.	6
FLEUR DE FLEURS	1/8oz.	30
FLEUR DE ROCAILLE	.1oz.	15
FLEUR DE ROCAILLE	1/16oz.	10
FLEUR SAUVAGE	.1oz.	30
FLIRTATION	1/8oz.	12
FLORIENT	1/16oz.	12
FOLLOW ME	1/8oz.	12
FORGET ME NOT	1/4oz.	10
FRACAS	.13oz.	8
FRANCETTE	.2oz.	35
FRENCH CANCAN	1/4oz.	50
FRENCH LILAC	1/4oz.	12
G GIGLI	1/4oz.	12
GALA NIGNT	1/6oz.	10
GALORE	1/2oz.	10
GARDENIA by Ashley	1/4oz.	10
GARDENIA by Cardinal	1/3oz.	7
GARDENIA		
by Duchess of Paris	1/8oz.	12
GARDENIA by Hollywood	1/8oz.	8
GARDENIA by Jergens	1/2oz.	9
GARDENIA by Jolind	.1oz.	8
GARDENIA		
by Arthur Philippi	1/4oz.	10
GARDENIA		
by Royal Perfumers	1/8oz.	12
GARDENIA by Stuart	1/2oz.	12
GARDENIA by Teel	1/2oz.	5
GARDENIA by Tre-jur	1/4oz.	15
GARDENIA PASSION	.26oz.	13
GEMEY	1/8oz.	20
GENNY SHINE	.16oz.	8
GIO	.17oz.	16
GIORGIO for men	1/8oz.	9
GLOBE for men	1/2oz.	13
GODDESS OF CRETE	nips	40
GOLD SATIN	1/8oz.	16
GOLDEN SHADOWS	1/6oz.	20
GOLDEN WOODS	1/16oz.	12
GRAND AMOUR	1/16oz.	8
GREAT LADY	1/4oz.	12
GREEN GODDESS	1/4oz.	25

Name	Size	Price
GUCCI for men	1/4oz.	5
HALSTON 1-12 for men	1/2oz.	13
HALSTON LIMITED for men	1/4oz.	5
HANADE	1/16oz.	7
HAWK for men	1/4oz.	5
HEAVEN SENT	1/2oz.	12
HENRI BENDEL	.13oz.	10
HO HANG for men	.3oz.	5
HONEY SUCKLE	1/2oz.	10
HOPE	1/16oz.	8
HOT	1/8oz.	11
HOYT Perfumer	1/4oz.	5
HOYT'S	1/4oz.	8
IL BACIO	1/8oz.	17
IMPERIAL DANISH MUSK	1/8oz.	5
IMPERIALE	1/4oz.	13
IMPREVU	1/16oz.	10
IMPREVU	1/8oz.	25
INDESCRET	1/4oz.	15
INDIAN SUMMER	1/2oz.	10
INFATLUT 07	1/8oz.	8
INOUI	1/4oz.	12
INSENSE for men	1/4oz.	8
INTERLUDE	1/16oz.	8
INTOXICATION	1/8oz.	8
INTOXICATION fluted glass	1/8oz.	20
IRICE bottle	1/4oz.	50
IRIS DE SENTEUS	1/8oz.	12
IRRESISTIBLE	1/5oz.	
	1/6oz.	12
JARDINS DE BAGATELLE	1/4oz.	17
JASMIN	.1oz.	20
JASMINE	1/4oz.	15
JE REVIENS	1/16oz.	
	1/6oz.	
	.236oz.	10/ea.
JEAN-PAUL GAULTIER torso	.1oz.	33
JEUNESSE	1/2oz.	7
JIL SANDER	1/4oz.	8
JIL SANDER FEELING MAN for men	1/4oz.	8
JODELLE	1/4oz.	8
JOLIE MADAME	1/16oz.	8
JONTUE	1/8oz.	8
JOOP! BERLIN	.17oz.	11

Name	Size	Price
JOOP! NIGHT FLIGHT for men	1/4oz.	10
JOOP! NUIT D'ETE	.17oz.	10
JOSEPH ABBOUD for men	.16oz.	10
JOY	.23oz.	30
JULES for men	1/3oz.	8
JUNGLE GARDENIA	1/16oz.	12
	.3oz.	8
K L	.17oz.	8
KANTARA	.14oz.	13
KASHAYA	.17oz.	20
L'AIMANT	1/2oz.	10
L'AIMANT	.65oz.	12
L'AIMANT	1/4oz.	14
L'AIR DU TEMPS	1/16oz.	50/ea.
L'EAU D'ISSEY	.1oz.	18
L'EFFLEUR	1/8oz.	7
L'HEURE BLEUE	.17oz.	20
L'ORIGAN creamy skin perfume	1/2oz.	5
L'UOMO GHERARDINI for men	1/5oz.	6
LA DEB	1/4oz.	6
LA NUIT DE NOEL	1/8oz.	25
LACOSTE for men	.14oz.	6
LADY CATHERINE	1/8oz.	10
LAGUNA	.17oz.	13
LALIQUE	.15oz.	20
LANCETTI ELLE	.17oz.	18
LAUREN	1/4oz.	12
LAVENDER SALTS	1/4oz.	20
LAZELL'S JOCKEY CLUB	app.1/4oz.	25
LE DIX	1/16oz.	12
LE PARFUM IDEAL	1/4oz.	100
LEADING LADY	1/8oz.	7
LENEL for men	1/8oz.	6
LEONARD DE LEONARD	1/8oz.	10
LES COPAINS	1/6oz.	13
LET'S DECIDE IT NOW	1/8oz.	6
LILAC	1/6oz.	12
LILAS 19	.13oz.	10
LILY	1/16oz.	10
LILY OF THE VALLEY by Colgate	1/8oz.	25
LILY OF THE VALLEY by Colgate	3/16oz.	8
LILY OF THE VALLEY by Ronni	1/4oz.	15/ea.

Name	Size	Price
LIMOUSINE for men	.17oz.	6
LINDA LEE	3/4oz.	8
LITTLE GREEN APPLE by Giftique	1/2oz.	7
LORE	1/8oz.	8
LOTUS	1/8oz.	10
LOTUS	1/16oz.	25
LOVABLE	1/8oz.	8
LOVE	1/2oz.	12
LUCIANO SOPRANI	.17oz.	15
LUCRETIA VANDERBILT	1/8oz.	25
LUZIER'S	1/8oz.	10
LYRA	.17oz.	19
MA GRIFFE	1/16oz.	12
MA GRIFFE	.17oz.	8
MACKIE	.17oz.	12
MADAME DE CARVEN	.16oz.	7
MADELEINE DE MADELEINE	.17oz.	6
MAGIE	1/8oz.	10
MAGNETIC	.1oz.	5
MAN BY JOVAN for men	1/2oz.	8
MARIELLA BURANI	.17oz.	19
MASUMI	1/8oz.	30
MEDITERRANEUM for men	1/4oz.	8
MELLOW-GLO	1/8oz.	8/ea.
MEMORIES	1/16oz.	5
MEN'S CLUB for men	1/8oz.	5
MIDNIGHT and OPTIMISTE	double	15
MILADY'S STRIKE	1/8oz.	25
MIMMINA	.17oz.	23
MING TOY	1/4oz.	25
MINOTAURE for men	1/6oz.	13
MISHA	.16oz.	14
MISS DIOR	.17oz.	16
MOLTO MISSONI	.12oz.	5
MONAD VIOLET	1/8oz.	20
MONSIEUR ROCHAS for men	1/8oz.	5
MONTANA D'ELLE	.08oz.	12
MONTANA for men	.13oz.	6
MUGUET DES BOIS	1/8oz.	8
MUGUET DU BONHEUR	1/8oz.	12
MUSE	1/16oz.	10
MY DESIRE	1/8oz.	6
MY SIN	1/4oz.	15

MY TREASURE	.12oz.	20	PINK SATIN	1/8oz.	8	SHANGHAI	1/2oz.	12
MYSTERE	1/8oz.	13	PIQUE	1/8oz.	10	SHEE-GWEE	1/4oz.	15
NAUGHTY	1/8oz.	8	PIVONE	1/4oz.	12	SHOCKING	1/16oz.	10
NINA	1/4oz.	45	POOLE'S PERFUME			SHOCKING YOU	3/4oz.	13
NINA	.20oz.	15	PRETENDERS II	.15oz.	5	SIKKIM	1/8oz.	10
NINJA	1/4oz.	10	POPPY MUSK	1/5oz.	6	SILENT NIGHT	1/4oz.	8
NINO CERRUTI	1/8oz.	13	POSSESSION	.1oz.	25	SINGAPORE NIGHTS	1/8oz.	25
NO REGRETS	.06oz.	10	POUR MONSIEUR			SIRENE	.2oz.	12
NOA NOA	.17oz.	13	for men	.13oz.	7	SIROCCO	.13oz.	15
NUIT D'ORCHIDEE	1/4oz.	12	PRESTIGE	1/4oz.	10	SOLO TU	.17oz.	13
NUIT DE LONGCHAMP	1/16oz.	15	PRINCESS MARINA			SONATA	1/4oz.	12
O DE LANCOME	1/4oz.	13	DE BOURBON	1/4oz.	23	SOURIRE FLEURI	1/4oz.	15
ODALISQUE	1/16oz.	12	PROPHECY	1/8oz.	8	SPARKLING GOLD	1/8oz.	8
OH LA LA by Azzaro	.1oz.	15	PUB for men	1/2oz.	5	SPICE	1/4oz.	10
OH LA LA by Ciro	1/16oz.	8	PURSENCE	.17oz.	11	SPICY APPLE BLOSSOM	1/8oz.	8
OMNI	1/2oz.	8	QUADRILLE	1/8oz.	15	STAMBOUL	1/4oz.	15
ON THE WIND	1/2oz.	8	QUELQUES FLEURS	1/2oz.	60	STRATEGY	1/4oz.	25
ONLY CRAZY	.3oz.	11	QUELQUES FLEURS	1/8oz.	20	STYX	1/4oz.	100
OPEN for men	.24oz.	10	RAFALE	1/16oz.	5	SUBLIME	.14oz.	18
OPERA 450	1/2oz.	15	RAPTURE	1/8oz.	13	SUEDE	1/8oz.	15
OPIUM	.12oz.	18	RED CARNATION	1/4oz.	8	SUN MOON STARS		
	1/4oz.	14	RED DOOR	.17oz.	12	LAGERFELD	.12oz.	25
ORANGE BLOSSOM			REGATTA for men	1/8oz.	5	SUNFLOWERS	1/4oz.	12
by Bo-Kay	1/8oz.	8	RELAX for men	1/4oz.	5	SURRENDER	.1oz.	20
ORANGE BLOSSOMS	1/2oz.	10	RENDEZVOUS	1/4oz.	12	SWEET PEA by Langlois	.1oz.	10
ORCHIDEE	1/4oz.	12	REPLIQUE	1/8oz.	65	SWEET PEA by Renaud	.1oz.	40
ORIENT	1/8oz.	7	REPLIQUE	1/16oz.	10	TABU	1/16oz.	40
PAILLETTES	.21oz.	5	Richard Hudnut bottle	.5 dram	15	TABU "HP"	1/16oz.	8
PAMYR	1/8oz.	8	ROMEO GIGLI for men	.17oz.	12	TAILSPIN	.15oz.	12
PANCALDI for men	.17oz.	7	ROSE	1/2oz.	50	TAJI	1/8oz.	5
PARCE QUE	1/16oz.	8	ROSES OF PLATINUM	1/8oz.	10	TENDRE POISON	.17oz.	20
PARFIQUE	1/4oz.	5	ROYAL PURPLE	1/3oz.	15	THEOSIRIS	.16oz.	23
PARFUM D'HERMES	1/6oz.	11	RUSSIAN LEATHER			TOCADE	.1oz.	20
PARIS by Coty	.13oz.	15	for men	1/2oz.	6	TODD OLDHAM	.2oz.	10
PARIS by YSL	1/4oz.	14	RUSSIAN perfume oil	vial	10	TORTUE	1/4oz.	8
PARURE	1/8oz.	12	RUSSIAN; RUSSE;			TOUCH	1/8oz.	20
PASCALLE	1/4oz.	10	RUSSICH	1/2oz.	25	TOUJOURS MOI	.12oz.	12
PASSION	.12oz.	11	SALVADOR DALI for men	.17oz.	8	TOUJOURS MOI	1/4oz.	50
PERFUME #1			SAMBA NOVA	1/2oz.	6	TOUJOURS MOI		
by Orgel Brothers		7	SAMPAQUITA	1/8oz.	12	by Max Factor	1/2oz.	35
Perfume Nips	tubes	5/ea.	SAYIDATY	.23oz.	13	TRES JOURDAN	.17oz.	17
PETAL MIST	1/8oz.	7	SCHERRER	1/8oz.	10	TRISTANO ONOFRI		10
PHANTOM for men	.17oz.	8	SCULPTURA	1/8oz.	30	TRUE LOVE	.12oz.	12
PHEROMONE	1/8oz.	18	SENCHAL	1/8oz.	8	TRULY LACE	1/8oz.	8
PHEROMONE			SERGIO SOLDANO			TRULY YOURS	1/2oz.	8
SACRED OIL	1/5oz.	20	for men	.2oz.	7	TRUSSARDI	1/4oz.	6
PHOTO for men	1/2oz.	13	SERGIO TACCHINI			TURBULENCES	1/14oz.	6
PINK PETALS	1/8oz.	8	for men	1/4oz.	8	TUSCANY PER DONNA	.12oz.	20

Name	Size	Price
TWEED	1/16oz.	
	1/8oz.	20
TWEED talc powder	3/4oz.	6
UGO VANELLI	.1oz.	12
UNE CARESSE	1/8oz.	75
VAN GILS for men	1/3oz.	7
VANDERBILT	.1oz.	8
VARIATIONS	1/16oz.	8
VENEZIA	.17oz.	17
VENICE	1/4oz.	12
VERSUS	.11oz.	8
VIA LANVIN	1/8oz.	15
VIE PRIVEE	1/4oz.	12
VIOLET SEC sachet	1-1/4oz.	5
VIOLET talc powder	1/2oz.	8
VIOLET WATER	1/8oz.	35
VIOLETTE DE PARME		
sachet	3/4oz.	5
VISION NOIR	1/4oz.	13
VIVID	1/8oz.	22
VIVONS	1/16oz.	10
VIVRE	1/16oz.	25
VOLAGE	1/8oz.	18
VOULEZ-VOUS	1/16oz.	8
WALLIS	1/3oz.	13
WHITE SATIN	1/8oz.	8
WHITE SHOULDERS		
by Evyan	1/8oz.	12
WHITE SHOULDERS		
by Evyan gold label	1/4oz.	25
WHITE SHOULDERS		
by Evyan heart shaped	1/4oz.	12
WHITE SHOULDERS		
by Evyan metal cased	1/6oz.	15/ea.
WHITE SHOULDERS		
by Evyan pillow	vial	8
WHITE SHOULDERS		
by Parfums Int. Ltd.	.12oz.	5
WHITE SHOULDERS		
by Parfums Int. Ltd.	1/4oz.	8
WILD HEART	.15oz.	5
WIND SONG	1/4oz.	9
WIND SONG scepter	1/4oz.	10
WINGS	1/8oz.	20
WITNESS for men	.13oz.	5
WOMENSWEAR		
by Alexander Julian	1/4oz.	12
X S for men	1/8oz.	10

Name	Size	Price
Y	1/16oz.	6
YANKY CLOVER	1/8oz.	12
YANKY CLOVER sachet	1-1/4oz.	5
YESTERDAY	1/4oz.	12
YOUTH-DEW	.12oz.	17
ZEGNA for men	.6oz.	10
ZIG ZAG	1/4oz.	5

AVON

Name	Size	Price
Avon Classic		
Perfume Collection	125oz. bottles	15
AVON FOR MEN	samples	10
AVON FRAGRANCES	Demonstrator	15
C'EST MOI!	.13oz.	7
CASBAH	.13oz.	7
FAR AWAY	.125oz.	12
LAHANA	.125oz.	7
NATORI	.13oz.	15
NIGHT MAGIC	.125oz.	7
Parisian Garden	.33oz.	5
Perfume Flaconette		90
PERLE NOIRE	.13oz.	7
Slipper Perfume	1/8oz.	10
TOPAZE	1/4oz.	50
TRAILING ARBUTUS	1/5oz.	5
VANILLA	.125oz.	7

NOVELTIES

Name	Size	Price
Devilbiss Perfumizers		15
Devilbiss pump atomizers		25
Miniature atomizer with funnel		6
Hand-blown glass bottle	Round	10
NARZISSE bottle	Pig	20
Sea shell decorated	5	
	Bottles	8/ea.
AFTER FIVE pendant	.09oz.	25
LITTLE GREEN APPLE		
pendant	1/8oz.	20
Black glass pendant	1/4oz.	13
Gold cased pendant		10
Perfume brooch		15
Needlepoint	1/8oz.	25
Tompadouc Viennese		
Handicraft	1/4oz.	20
Needlepoint	1/8oz.	
	1/4oz.	25/ea.

Name	Size	Price
Brass bottle and brass cap		50
Czechoslovakia bottle,		
Czechoslovakia		95
Silver overlay flacon	1/8oz.	25
Glided rose bottle	.10oz.	8
Ballerina decorated bottle	1/4oz.	8
Perfume purse flacon	1/4oz.	6
Boutique purse flacon	1 dram	25
ORANGE BLOSSOM		
in shoe	.1oz.	35
FLORALE telephone	.5 dram	25
GALA NIGHT		
hurricane candle bottle	.10oz.	15
Hurricane oil lamp	1/8oz.	10
Perfume Hi-lights	1/2 dram	
	bottles	85
CABBAGE PATCH KIDS	1/2oz.	6
BOUQUET	1/2oz.	15
HEAVEN candle and		
APPLE BLOSSOM candle		
in angel	1/8oz.	15
Sophisti-Cats	1/8oz.	10/ea.

PERFUME BOTTLE SETS

Name	Size	Price
Colgates Miniature Size		
Extracts	5 bottles	50
Miniature Perfumes		
by Colgate	3 bottles	45
Flowers of the Evening	3 bottles	25
Book of Perfume	3 bottles	50
Duvinne glass ball	3 bottles	75
Perfume Collection		
by Prince Matchabelli	3 bottles	40
Ivel Perfumes	3 bottles	30
Evan's Two Golden Hearts	2 bottles	75
Perfumed writing sets		
by Chanel	2 pens	20/set
Exquisit 750	5 bottles	50
Cosmopolitan's Collection		
of International Famous		
Perfumes	10 bottles	95
Nina Ricci set	5 bottles	95
Elizabeth Taylor's		
Fragrant Jewel Collection	4 bottles	25
Small Wonders	5 bottles	25
Fragrant Treasures	10 bottles	50

Parfum House / Fragrance

PARFUM HOUSE	FRAGRANCE
Ahrc	LOVE
Albin du Roy	KANTARA
Jean D'Albret	CASAQUE
Angelique	GOLD SATIN
Angelique	PINK SATIN
Angelique	WHITE SATIN
Anucci	DALINI
Annette	ORANGE BLOSSOMS
Aramis Inc.	ARAMIS
Aramis Inc.	ARAMIS 900
Aramis Inc.	TUSCANY PER DONNA
Elizabeth Arden Co.	BLUE GRASS
Elizabeth Arden Co.	CABRIOLE
Elizabeth Arden Co.	OPERA 450
Elizabeth Arden Co.	RED DOOR
Elizabeth Arden Co.	SUNFLOWERS
Elizabeth Arden Co.	TRUE LOVE
Giorgio Armani Parfums	ARMANI
Giorgio Armani Parfums	GIO
Ashley	GARDENIA
Associated Distributor Inc.	CHEN YU FLOWERING ALMOND
Associated Merchandising Corp	JODELLE
Atkins Ltd.	SHEE-GWEE
Parfums Aubusson	DESIRADE
Auvergne Et Cie, Inc.	AFTER FIVE
Avon Products, Inc.	AVON LEATHER
Avon Products, Inc.	BIRD OF PARADISE
Avon Products, Inc.	BRAVO
Avon Products, Inc.	C'EST MOI!
Avon Products, Inc.	CASBAH
Avon Products, Inc.	CHARISMA
Avon Products, Inc.	COTILLION
Avon Products, Inc.	DEEP WOODS
Avon Products, Inc.	FAR AWAY
Avon Products, Inc.	FIELD FLOWERS
Avon Products, Inc.	HERE'S MY HEART
Avon Products, Inc.	IMARI
Avon Products, Inc.	IMPERIAL GARDEN
Avon Products, Inc.	LAHANA
Avon Products, Inc.	MESMERIZE
Avon Products, Inc.	MOONWIND
Avon Products, Inc.	NATORI
Avon Products, Inc.	NIGHT MAGIC
Avon Products, Inc.	OCCUR!
Avon Products, Inc.	OLAND
Avon Products, Inc.	PATCHWORK
Avon Products, Inc.	PERLE NOIRE
Avon Products, Inc.	ROSES, ROSES
Avon Products, Inc.	SOFT MUSK
Avon Products, Inc.	SONNET
Avon Products, Inc.	SPICY
Avon Products, Inc.	TAI WINDS
Avon Products, Inc.	TO A WILD ROSE
Avon Products, Inc.	TOPAZE
Avon Products, Inc.	TRAILING ARBUTUS
Avon Products, Inc.	TRIBUTE
Avon Products, Inc.	UFORGETTABLE
Avon Products, Inc.	VANILLA
Avon Products, Inc.	WINDJAMMER
Loris Azzaro	OH LA LA
Babcock	LORE
J.S. Bach	SONATA
Balenciaga	HO HANG
Balenciaga	LE DIX
Balenciaga	QUADRILLE
Parfums Balmain	JOLIE MADAME
Jean Barthet	BIBI
Parfums Mikhail Baryshinikov	MISHA
Robert Beaulieu Parfums	VISION NOIR
Parfums L.V. Beethoven	BEETHOVEN
Henri Bendel	BENDELILAS
Henri Bendel	HENRI BENDEL
Henri Bendel	SUEDE
Franka M. Berger	COEUR DE CANANGA
Poly Bergen Cosmetics	TORTUE
Bernard Perfumer	MEMORIES
Laura Biagiotti	BIAGIOTTI
Laura Biagiotti	VENEZIA
Bijan	DNA
Blair	LA DEB
A. Blanc	BAVARDAGE
A. Blanc	CITANA
Parfums Jacques Bogart	BOIS DE VETIVER
Parfums Jacques Bogart	WITNESS
Bo-Kay Perfumer	MY DESIRE
Bo-Kay Perfumer	ORANGE BLOSSOM
Bonjour Parfums, Inc.	BONJOUR
Guy Bouchara	THEOSIRIS
Bourjois	EVENING IN PARIS
Bourjois	ON THE WIND
Bouton	GALA NIGHT
Bouton	LILY
Mariella Burani	MARIELLA BURANI
California Perfume Co.	TRAILING ARBUTUS
Parfums Capucci	PARSE QUE
Pierre Cardin	CARDIN
Cardinal	BOUQUET
Cardinal	CHYPRE
Cardinal	GARDENIA
Cardinal	ORIENT
Carme Int'l. Inc.	POPPY MUSK
Hattie Carnegie	CARNEGIE PINK
Parfums Caron	BELLODGIA
Parfums Caron	FLEUR DE ROCAILLE
Parfums Caron	FRENCH CANCAN
Parfums Caron	LA NUIT DE NOEL
Parfums Caron	MUGUET DU BONHEUR
Parfums Carven	MA GRIFFE
Parfums Carven	MADAME DE CARVEN
Parfums Carven	VARIATIONS
Pridu Cebehrsk	CREDO
Parfums Nino Cerruti	NINO CERRUTI
Champrel	SPICE
Chanel	CHANEL NO 5
Chanel	COCO
Chanel	EGOISTE PLATINUM
Chanel	POUR MONSIEUR
Charbert	BREATHLESS
Charles V	1800
Charles V	CORDON D'OR
Charles V	CROYANCE
Charles V	PAMYR
Charles of the Ritz	SENCHAL
Chaurand	HANADE
Cheramy	APRIL SHOWERS
Cheramy	IRIS DE SENTEUS
Mary Chess	GARDENIA
Mary Chess	STRATEGY
Mary Chess	WHITE LILAC
Parfums Ciro	OH LA LA
Parfums Ciro	SURRENDER
Liz Claiborne Cosmetics, Inc.	CLAIBORNE
Liz Claiborne Cosmetics, Inc.	VIVID
Clairns	ELYSIUM
L. Clavel	GRAND AMOUR
Parfums de Coeur	NINJA
Colgate	FLORIENT
Colgate	FLORIENT FLOWERS OF THE ORIENT
Colgate & Co.	CAPRICE
Colgate & Co.	CASHMERE BOUQUET
Colgate & Co.	DACTYLIS
Colgate & Co.	LA FRANCE ROSE
Colgate & Co.	LILY OF THE VALLEY
Colgate & Co.	MONAD VIOLET
Colgate & Co.	VIOLET WATER
Colgate Palmolive-Peet Co.	LILY OF THE VALLEY
Congoleum Corp.	PRESTIGE
Parfums Corday Inc.	FAME
Parfums Corday Inc.	POSSESSION
Parfums Corday Inc.	TOUJOURS MOI
Parfums Carlo Corinto	CARLO CORINTO ROUGE
Coty, Inc.	EMERAUDE
Coty, Inc.	L'AIMANT
Coty, Inc.	L'EFFLEUR
Coty, Inc.	LIPAS POURPRE
Coty, Inc.	L'ORIGAN
Coty, Inc.	MUGUET DES BOIS
Coty, Inc.	MUSE
Coty, Inc.	PARIS
Coty, Inc.	STYX
Coty, Inc.	TRULY LACE

Coty Division of Pfizer	EMERAUDE
Coty Division of Pfizer	IMPREVU
Coty Division of Pfizer	L'AIMANT
Coty Division of Pfizer	MASUMI
Courreges Parfums	EMPREINTE
Enrico Coveri	PAILLETTES
Daggett & Ramsdell	DEBONAIR
Daggett & Ramsdell	SPARKLING GOLD
Parfums Salvador Dali	LAGUNA
Parfums Salvador Dali	SALVADOR DALI
Dana Parfums Corp.	CANOE
Dana Parfums Corp.	EMIR
Dana Parfums Corp.	TABU
Parfums Davidoff	RELAX
Deborah Int'l. Beauty, Ltd.	OMNI
Parfums Alain Delon	LYRA
Deltah Perfumes, Inc.	CHYPRE
Deltah Perfumes, Inc.	RENDEZVOUS
DeMarsay, Inc.	JASMIN
Francis Denney	HOPE
Francis Denney	INTERLUDE
Diana De Silva Cosmetics	GENNY SHINE
Diana De Silva Cosmetics	LES COPAINS
Parfums Christian Dior	DIORESSENCE
Parfums Christian Dior	JULES
Parfums Christian Dior	MISS DIOR
Parfums Christian Dior	TENDRE POISON
Parfum D'or de Paris	CHARMANTE
D'Orsay	DIVINE
D'Orsay	INTOXICATION
D'Orsay	VOULEY-VOUS
DuBe	UNKNOWN
Duchess of Paris	GARDENIA
Duchess of Paris	INFATLUT 07
Duchess of Paris	NAUGHTY
Duchess of Paris	SINGAPORE NIGHTS
Alfred Dunhill Ltd.	DUNHILL
Duleve	ALORS
Duvinne	CARNATION
Duvinne	GARDENIA
Duvinne	LILAC
Perry Ellis	360
Eurocos	BOSS
Euroitalia	DOLCE & GABBANA
Euroitalia	JOSEPH ABBOUD
Parfums Evyan	GOLDEN SHADOWS
Parfums Evyan	GREAT LADY
Parfums Evyan	MOST PRECIOUS
Parfums Evyan	WHITE SHOULDERS
Faberge, Inc.	BRUT 33
Faberge, Inc.	FLANBEAU
Jacques Fath Parfums	ELLIPSE
Jacques Fath Parfums	EXPRESSION
Jacques Fath Parfums	FATH DE FATH
Fendi	ASJA
Alberta Ferretti	FEMINA
Finesse, Inc.	FINESSE
De Fontenay	BAHAMOUR
Forcelli Co.	PETAL MIST
Forest Parfumery	MING TOY
The Fuller Brush Co.	APPLE BLOSSOM
The Fuller Brush Co.	LEADING LADY
The Fuller Brush Co.	REGATTA
Le Galion	BOURRASQUE
Le Galion	JASMINE
Parfums Jean-Paul Gaultier	JEAN-PAUL

	GAULTIER
Parfums Gherardini	DONNA
Parfums Gherardini	L'UOMO GHERARDINI
Giftique	LITTLE GREEN APPLE
Giorgio Armani Parfums	ARMANI
Giorgio Beverly Hills	CLASSIC MATCH
Giorgio Beverly Hills	GIORGIO
Giorgio Beverly Hills	WINGS
Parfums Givenchy	INSENSE
Annick Goutal	EAU DE CHARLOTTE
Annick Goutal	GARDENIA PASSION
Grafton Products Corp.	CHALEUR
Parfums Gres	CABOCHARD
Parfums Gres	CABOTINE
Guerlain Parfums	CHAMADE
Guerlain Parfums	IMPERIALE
Guerlain Parfums	JARDINS DE BAGATELLE
Guerlain Parfums	L'HEURE BLEUE
Guerlain Parfums	PARURE
Halston Fragrances, Inc.	CATALYST
Halston Fragrances, Inc.	HALSTON 1-12
Halston Fragrances, Inc.	HALSTON LIMITED
Fred Hayman Beverly Hills	TOUCH
Gale Hayman Inc.	BEVERLY HILLS
Gale Hayman Inc.	DELICIOUS
The Herb Farm Shop Ltd.	ROYAL PURPLE
Parfums Hermes	PARFUM D'HERME'S
Hess	RED CARNATION
The Higbee Co. of Faberge	FABERGE
Houbigant	CHANTILLY
Houbigant	INDIAN SUMMER
Houbigant	LE PARFUM IDEAL
Houbigant	QUELQUES FLEURS
Hove	FLAME
Howe Co. Inc.	BOUQUET SUPREME
Howe Co. Inc.	GARDENIA
Hoyt Co. Inc.	HOYT'S THE ORIGINAL 1868
Hoyt	STAMBOUL
Richard Hudnut	GEMEY
Richard Hudnut	VIOLET SEC SACHET
Richard Hudnut	YANKY CLOVER
Richard Hudnut	YANKY CLOVER SACHET
Imperial Del Oro	RUSSIAN LEATHER
Intercosma	SERGIO SOLDANO
Intercosma West	MIMMINA
Irresistible	IRRESISTIBLE
Isabey	SOURIRE FLEURI
Ivel	CHYPRE
Ivel	GARDENIA
Ivel	MON DESIR
Parfums Jamaica	FORGET ME NOT
Parfums Jamaica	JEUNESSE
Jergens	BEN HUR
Jergens	GARDENIA
Jolind	GARDENIA
Parfums Joop!	JOOP! BERLIN
Parfums Joop!	JOOP! NIGHT FLIGHT
Parfums Joop!	JOOP! NUIT D'ETE
Joubert	BLUE WALTZ
Parfums Charles Jourdan	TRES JOURDAN
Jovan Inc.	MAN BY JOVAN
Jovan Inc.	SCULPTURA
Alexander Julian	WOMENSWEAR BY ALEXANDER JULIAN
Kenzo	KASHAYA
Otto Kern	NOA NOA

Anne Klein	BLAZER
Calvin Klein Cosmetics Corp.	CALVIN KLEIN
Calvin Klein Cosmetics Corp.	C K ONE
Calvin Klein Cosmetics Corp.	ETERNITY
Kensington Inc.	PASCALLE
Keystone Perfume Co.	LAVENDER SALTS
Christian Lacroix	C'EST LA VIE!
Bernard Lalande	AMBRE
Bernard Lalande	IRISE
Bernard Lalande	VERT
Lalique Parfums	LALIQUE
Lancetti	LANCETTI ELLE
Parfums Lancome	MAGIE
Parfums Lancome	O DE LANCOME
Parfums Lancome	SIKKIM
Lander Co. Inc.	BOUQUET
Lander Co. Inc.	HEAVEN
Lander Co. Inc.	PINK PETALS
Lander Co. Inc.	SPICY APPLE BLOSSOM
Lander Co. Inc.	TRULY YOURS
Langlois	SWEET PEA
Parfums Lanvin	ARPEGE
Parfums Lanvin	MY SIN
Parfums Lanvin	VIA LANVIN
Parfums Ted Lapidus	FANTASME
Estee Lauder	ALIAGE FRAGRANCE
Estee Lauder	AZUREE FRAGRANCE
Estee Lauder	BEAUTIFUL
Estee Lauder	CINNABAR
Estee Lauder	ESTEE SUPER PERFUME
Estee Lauder	KNOWING
Estee Lauder	PRIVATE COLLECTION
Estee Lauder	SPELLBOUND
Estee Lauder	WHITE LINEN
Estee Lauder	YOUTH-DEW
Parfums Ralph Lauren	LAUREN
Yves Saint Laurent Parfums	CHAMPAGNE
Yves Saint Laurent Parfums	OPIUM
Yves Saint Laurent Parfums	PARIS
Yves Saint Laurent Parfums	Y
Lazell's	JOCKEY CLUB
Leigh	DESERT FLOWER
Lucien Lelong	INDISCRET
Lucien Lelong	SIROCCO
Lucien Lelong	TAILSPIN
Lentheric Perfumes	CONFETTI
Lentheric Perfumes	SHANGHAI
Lentheric Perfumes	TWEED
Lentheric Perfumes	TWEED TALC
Lenel Perfumes Inc.	LENNEL
Leonard Parfums	FASHION
Leonard Parfums	LEONARD DE LEONARD
Liz Taylor	DIAMONDS AND EMERALDS
Liz Taylor	DIAMONDS AND RUBIES
Liz Taylor	DIAMONDS AND SAPHIRES
Liz Taylor	PASSION
Liz Taylor	WHITE DIAMONDS
Parfum L'Orle,Inc.	LILAS 19 L'ORLE
Lovable Cosmetics Inc.	LOVABLE
Lubin	NUIT DE LONGCHAMP
Luciano Profumi	LUCIANO SOPRANI
Luziers Inc.	LUZIER'S
Lynette	FANTASIA
Bob Mackie	MACKIE
Madeleine Mono Ltd.	MADELEINE DE MADELEINE

Mas Cosmetics .... ONLY CRAZY
Marbert .... YESTERDAY
Neiman Marcus .... VOLAGE
Princess Marina de Bourbon . PRINCESS MARINA DE BOURBON
Countess Maritza .... SILENT NIGHT
Alexander de Markoff, Ltd. .... ENIGMA
Alexander de Markoff, Ltd. .... NO REGRETS
House of Martens .... GARDENIA
House of Martens .... LAVENDER
House of Martens .... VIOLET
Max Factor .... EPRIS
Max Factor .... GOLDEN WOODS
Max Factor .... HYPNOTIQUE
Max Factor .... LITTLE GREEN APPLE
Max Factor .... TOUJOURS MOI
The Mennen Co. .... HAWK
Marilyn Miglin .... PHEROMONE
Marilyn Miglin .... PHEROMONE SACRED OIL
Missoni .... MOLTO MISSONI
Parfums Issey Miyake .... L'EAU D'ISSEY
Parfums Molinard .... CONCRETA MUGUET
Parfums Molinard .... RAFALE
Molyneux .... VIVRE
Mondi .... PURSENCE
Claude Montana Parfums .... MONTANA
Claude Montana Parfums .... MONTANA D'ELLE
Germaine Monteil Cosmetics Corp .... BAKIR
Germaine Monteil Cosmetics Corp .... CHAMPAGNE
Germaine Monteil Cosmetics Corp .... FLEUR SAUVAGE
Germaine Monteil Cosmetics Corp .... GALORE BATH PERFUME
Morris .... SERGIO TACCHINNI
Muelhens Inc. .... MAGNETIC
Thierry Mugler Parfums .... ANGEL
Merle Norman Cosmetics .... DECOLLETE
Merle Norman Cosmetics .... VIVONS
Oberon .... UNE CARESSE
Tristano Onofri .... SOLO TU
Tristano Onofri .... TRISTANO ONOFRI
Orgel Brothers .... PERFUME #1
Original Appalachian Artworks Inc .... CABBAGE PATCH KIDS
Parfums International Ltd. .... CHLOE
Parfums International Ltd. .... K L
Parfums International Ltd. .... PHOTO
Parfums International Ltd. .... SUN MOON STARS LAGERFELD
Parfums International Ltd. . WHITE SHOULDERS
Park & Tilford .... ADVENTURE
Park & Tilford .... CHERISH
Park & Tilford .... DESIRE
Park & Tilford .... HONEY SUCKLE
Parlux Fragrances, Inc. .... LIMOUSINE
Parlux Fragrances, Inc. .... PHANTOM
Parlux Fragrances, Inc. .... SIRENE
Parlux Fragrances, Inc. .... TODD OLDHAM
Jean Patou Parfumer 1000
Jean Patou Parfumer .... COCKTAIL DRY
Jean Patou Parfumer .... JOY
Jean Patou Parfumer .... SUBLIME

The Perfumer's Workshop, Ltd. . ...SAMBA NOVA
Dorothy Perkins Co., Inc.   ROSES OF PLATINUM
Arthur Philippi .... ENGLISH SPICE
Arthur Philippi .... GARDENIA
Parfums Paloma Picasso .... MINOTAURE
Parfums Robert Piguet .... BANDIT
Parfums Robert Piguet .... CALYPSO
Parfums Robert Piguet .... FRACAS
Ed Pinaud .... CEDRAT
Ed Pinaud .... FLIRTATION
Pitkin Inc. .... LINDA LEE
Poole's Beauty Boutique .... POOLE'S PERFUME PRETENDERS II
Prestige Fragrances, Ltd. .... HOT
Prince Matchabelli, Inc. .... ABANO
Prince Matchabelli, Inc. .... ABANO BATH OIL
Prince Matchabelli, Inc. .... AVIANCE
Prince Matchabelli, Inc. AVIANCE NIGHT MUSK
Prince Matchabelli, Inc. .... BELOVED
Prince Matchabelli, Inc. .... CACHET
Prince Matchabelli, Inc. .... CROWN JEWEL
Prince Matchabelli, Inc. .... PROPHECY
Prince Matchabelli, Inc. .... STRADIVARI
Prince Matchabelli, Inc. .... WIND SONG
Princess Marcella Borghese .... IL BACIO
Parfums Princesse Wallis. .... WALLIS
Proteo .... MEDITERRANEUM
Proteo .... G GIGLI
Proteo .... ROMEO GIGLI
Emilio Pucci .... VIVARA
Pupa Parfums .... FIORILU
Parfums Paco Rabanne .... X S
Raphael .... REPLIQUE
Redken Labs Inc. .... PIQUE
Renaud .... SWEET PEA
Maison Renee .... ALINE
Parfums Revillon .... DETCHEMA
Parfums Revillon .... TURBULENCES
Revlon .... JONTUE
Revlon .... PUB
Revlon .... WILD HEART
I.W. Rice .... I.W. RICE
Parfums Nina Ricci .... BIGARADE
Parfums Nina Ricci .... CAPRICCI
Parfums Nina Ricci .... COEUR JOIE
Parfums Nina Ricci .... FAROUCHE
Parfums Nina Ricci .... FLEUR DE FLEURS
Parfums Nina Ricci .... L'AIR DU TEMPS
Parfums Nina Ricci .... NINA
Rieger Parfumer .... FRANCETTE
Rilling Dermetics Co. .... GODDESS OF CRETE
Rivara Division Hanorah .... PANCALDI
Robinson Cosmetics Co. .... FLORALE
Parfums Rochas .... EAU DE ROCHAS
Parfums Rochas .... GLOBE
Parfums Rochas .... MONSIEUR ROCHAS
Parfums Rochas .... MYSTERE
Parfums Rochas .... TOCADE
Yves Rocher .... 8e JOUR
Yves Rocher .... NUIT D'ORCHIDEE
Yves Rocher .... ORCHIDEE
Yves Rocher .... PIVOINE
Yves Rocher .... VENICE

Yves Rocher .... VIE PRIVEE
Roger & Gallet ..... BLUE CARNATION SACHET
Roger & Gallet .... OPEN
Roger & Gallet .. VIOLETT DE PARME SACHET
Parfums Ronni .... LILY OF THE VALLEY
Nettie Rosenstein .... ODALISQUE
De Rothschild Ltd. .... EXOTIC MUSK
Frances Rothschild, Inc. .... AMBER
Frances Rothschild, Inc. .... DE ROTHSCHILD
Royal Perfumers Inc. .... GARDENIA
Parfums Helena Rubinstein .... BARYNIA
Parfums Helena Rubinstein .... COURANT
Parfums Helena Rubinstein .... EMOTION
Parfums Helena Rubinstein .... HEAVEN SENT
Parfums Helena Rubinstein .... MEN'S CLUB
Russia .... RUSSIAN PERFUME OIL
Jil Sander Cosmetics .... FEELING MAN
Jil Sander Cosmetics .... JIL SANDER
Sayidaty .... SAYIDATY
Scandia Int'l. Ltd. .... IMPERIAL DANISH MUSK
Parfums Jean-Louis Scherrer .... SCHERRER
Parfums Schiaparelli .... DANCE ARROGANCE
Parfums Schiaparelli .... SHOCKING
Parfums Schiaparelli .... SHOCKING YOU
Schissler's Perfume .... EXTRA
Paul Sebastian .... DESIGN
C.H. Selick .... APPLE BLOSSOM
Shiseido Cosmetics .... INOUI
Shulton .... TAJI
Parfum Similaire Inc. .... PARFIQUE
Sofipar Int'l. Inc. .... LACOSTE
Speidel .... BRITISH STERLING
Spencer Perfume Co. .... ROSE
Stanley Home Products .... LADY CATHERINE
Bruno Storp .... RUSSE RUSSISCH
Stuart Perfumer .... GARDENIA
Stuart Products Co. .... MILADY'S STRIKE
Teel .... GARDENIA
Tre-Jur .... GARDENIA
Treasure Masters Perfume .... MY TREASURE
Trussardi Parfums .... TRUSSARDI
Tussy, Len & Fink Products Corp......MIDNIGHT
Tussy, Len & Fink Products Corp......OPTIMISTE
Tuvache .... JUNGLE GARDENIA
Gloria Vanderbilt .... VANDERBIILT
Lucretia Vanderbilt .... ALURIA
Lucretia Vanderbilt .... LUCRETIA VANDERBILT
Parfums Ugo Vanelli .... UGO VANELLI
Van Gils Cosmetics .... VAN GILS
Varva .... FOLLOW ME
Veldez .... GREEN GODDESS
Parfums Jean-louis Vermeil .... CASAQUE
Gianni Versace .... VERSUS
Victoria Secret .... RAPTURE
Adrienne Vittadini .... A V
J.B. Williams Co. .... VIOLET TALC
Parfums Worth .... JE REVIENS
Wrisley .... FRENCH LILAC
Yardley .... APRIL VIOLETS SACHET
Yardley .... LOTUS
Ermenegildo Zegna .... ZEGNA
Zsa Zsa .... ZIG ZAG

Fragrance / Parfum House / Index